Mindfulness Training

A Beginners Guide to Expand Your Mind Power and Develop Mental Toughness

(How to Keep Your Attention With Mindfulness Techniques)

Nathan Deluca

Published by Rob Miles

© **Nathan Deluca**

All Rights Reserved

Mindfulness Training: A Beginners Guide to Expand Your Mind Power and Develop Mental Toughness (How to Keep Your Attention With Mindfulness Techniques)

ISBN 978-1-990084-05-8

All rights reserved. No part of this guide may be reproduced in any form without permission in writing from the publisher except in the case of brief quotations embodied in critical articles or reviews.

Legal & Disclaimer

The information contained in this book is not designed to replace or take the place of any form of medicine or professional medical advice. The information in this book has been provided for educational and entertainment purposes only.

The information contained in this book has been compiled from sources deemed reliable, and it is accurate to the best of the Author's knowledge; however, the Author cannot guarantee its accuracy and validity and cannot be held liable for any errors or omissions. Changes are periodically made to this book. You must consult your doctor or get professional medical advice before using any of the suggested remedies, techniques, or information in this book.

Upon using the information contained in this book, you agree to hold harmless the Author from and against any damages, costs, and expenses, including any legal fees potentially resulting from the application of any of the information provided by this guide. This disclaimer applies to any damages or injury caused by the use and application, whether directly or indirectly, of any advice or information presented, whether for breach of contract, tort, negligence, personal injury, criminal intent, or under any other cause of action.

You agree to accept all risks of using the information presented inside this book. You need to consult a professional medical practitioner in order to ensure you are both able and healthy enough to participate in this program.

Table of Contents

INTRODUCTION 1

CHAPTER 1: THE TROUBLES THAT HOUND YOU 4

CHAPTER 2: TECHNIQUES USED IN MINDFULNESS MEDITATION 13

CHAPTER 3: COMING FACE TO FACE WITH YOURSELF 17

CHAPTER 4: ABOUT MINDFULNESS 20

CHAPTER 5: WHAT IS MINDFULNESS MEDITATION? 29

CHAPTER 6: POSTURES TO PRACTICE MINDFULNESS 34

CHAPTER 7: DEFINING MINDFULNESS 37

CHAPTER 8: WHAT IS MINDFULNESS? 46

CHAPTER 9: USING MINDFULNESS TO BECOME HAPPIER, PEACEFUL, AND FOCUSED 52

CHAPTER 10: MINDFULNESS DEFINED 62

CHAPTER 11: WHAT IS MINDFULNESS? 70

CHAPTER 12: UNDERSTANDING MINDFULNESS 75

CHAPTER 13: MINDFULNESS 78

CHAPTER 14: MINDFULNESS 87

CHAPTER 15: WHAT IS MINDFULNESS? 94

CHAPTER 16: THE SECRETS TO ELIMINATE DISTRACTIONS 104

CHAPTER 17: LIVING A HEALTHIER LIFESTYLE- MAKING MINDFUL CHOICES 110

CHAPTER 18: 7 DAYS OF MINDFULNESS 125

CHAPTER 19: MINDFULNESS MEDITATION TECHNIQUES 128

CHAPTER 20: GETTING TO KNOW MINDFULNESS 144

CHAPTER 21: FORMAL MEDITATION 151

CHAPTER 22: HOW TO PRACTICE MINDFULNESS. 160

CHAPTER 23: EATING MINDFULLY 169

CHAPTER 24: MEDITATION TO INCREASE HAPPINESS 176

CHAPTER 25: HOW YOUR THOUGHTS AFFECT HOW YOU FEEL 184

CHAPTER 26: STEPPING INTO THE WORLD 192

CHAPTER 27: DEALING WITH CONCENTRATION ISSUES. 197

CONCLUSION 205

Introduction

I am not sure how advanced you are in knowing about Mindfulness. I am going to assume that you don't know very much about it because I always feel that it's important to know from A to Z when you are learning something new. You will see from the title that you will be asked to be more positive, but mindfulness is a lot more than that. It's a way of life and once you accept it as YOUR way of life, you will find that life takes on a new twist and you start to feel happy in your life.

What causes this happiness is being able to detach yourself from things that have happened to you. With so much unhappiness in the world, it's not surprising that the figures for prescription drugs used in the case of anxiety and stress are on the up. When you consider medical technology, one would assume that if more drugs were being prescribed, surely the figures of people suffering from stress would fall, but the opposite has happened. Stress is a major problem. It was thought that it would be beneficial for scientists and medical experts to work with Buddhist monks who are accustomed to living mindful lives to see what difference there was in their lifestyle and that of people who display stress. What was found was very interesting in that the creative side of the brain is used just as much as the calculating side of the brain.

Doctors then went on to see how mindfulness affects people. Work that took place between the Dalai Lama and medical experts came up with the conclusion that many new cases of stress and anxiety should be treated with mindfulness as opposed to anti-anxiety drugs. This is something that has been done over the past couple of years in the United Kingdom and the results are showing vast improvements. This is why mindfulness is so important to understand. Much of what you are asked to do in classes are things that you can do on your own. Thus, this book will help you with your first journey into the new world of mindfulness.

Chapter 1: The Troubles That Hound You

Practicing meditation and mindfulness is a personal journey. It is a simple, practical, subtle, and yet deeply transformative experience. The journey can be different with everyone, as any person can choose to take a different path for his or her own reasons. However, if done regularly and with sincerity, the physical, mental, and spiritual benefits abound for everyone.

This ancient Buddhist practice, along with other Buddhist philosophies, has been gaining ground in the modern world. It seems as if the people of today are looking for alternative ways to handle and cope with the problems that they have to face daily. Certainly, meditation and mindfulness offer a wholly different way of managing stress and finding happiness, and millions of people have found it effective. But before you can start to learn how meditation can help you, you first have to know what aspect of your life you need help with and delve into the stressors that have a tendency to exhaust you.

Stress and Modern Man

Stress has become a daily staple in this fast-paced, materialistic world. Hundreds of millions of people struggle with depression and anxiety and the numbers rise every day. Worse of all, it has become the norm to live mechanically, going through life rather than truly experiencing it.

There have probably been plenty of times that you've felt stressed and overwhelmed by everything in your life, whether it is your job, your relationships, or your personal, inner life. There are many factors that contribute or cause stress and it's important to root out yours.

High-standards and the Desire for the Ideal

All your life, societal standards, the media, your personal experiences, as well as education have all helped form an image of what life should be and who you're supposed to be. These expectations may already be in place before you were even born, such as expectations from you parents, or the conditioning you get every day from mainstream media that tells you how and who you should be. Expectations and standards like these can cause a lot of stress for the people who are led to believe that anything less is not worth having.

Your personal desire to reach a certain ideal can also be a huge cause of stress. This ideal can be the image of a white picket fence in a great neighborhood with kids playing in the front yard, it could be a million-dollar condo and an expensive car, or it might even just be the image of the perfect, romantic couple.

This ideal can encompass your whole way of life up to the smallest detail. Whatever image it is for you, this ideal becomes the standard of comparison. You end up striving so hard to reach and achieve this ideal or standard that you miss out on simple pleasures.

Coping with Regretful Mistakes and Mortifying Failure

Mistakes and failures have to be faced throughout life. No one in the world, no matter how successful, is immune to facing failure. Inspirational ads may lead you to believe that you can do anything you set your mind to, but the reality is you will have to face your fair share of failure. Having your carefully laid out plans fall apart before your eyes can be devastating and people are rarely ready to cope with it.

Most of the time, when you're faced with the mistakes you make, you end up being overly critical and even hateful towards yourself. You start to lose confidence in your capabilities and you become afraid to assert yourself because you might end up just making another mistake.

The Desire to be in Control

In this world of uncertainty, it is sometime a great comfort to think that you, at least, have a fair amount of control in your own life. After all, you're the one who makes decisions in your life and no one else, right? Control, however, is a very tenuous state of being. Control might be in your hands one minute, then gone the next.

You can plan your day up to the last minute and still get all your plans derailed by traffic or bad weather. The fact is that no matter how hard you strive for control, you just can't control everything.

Alienation and isolation

Urban life can seem like a constant rat-race form one thing to the next. So many people are packed together in such a small space that you would expect a lot more connections being made, but the opposite is true. Life in the city can be very lonely, and a lot of people feel alienated.

This is especially true nowadays with employment and work becoming more specialized and outsourced. There is very little time and opportunity to form bonds or connections. A lot of people feel like they're just floating from one situation to the next without a clear anchor or a clear idea of where they want to be headed. Advancements in technology and communication have made the world "smaller" but have also left a lot of people feeling fragmented and disconnected.

Happiness in All the Wrong Places

The biggest problem that people have to face is how to cope with these stressors and how to actually be happy while doing their jobs and living their life. However, modern society also has its own version of what equates happiness and what happiness *should* look like. Of course, this doesn't work for everyone, and even when it does, it still doesn't work for long.

Consumerism

In a society that feeds on profit, you are always encouraged to spend and acquire more and more possessions. You are led to believe that having an excess of everything is the key to being happy. Being able to afford everything you want, regardless of whether you actually need it or not, have become the ideal. You get a thrill when you buy something new, you feel happy and good about yourself.

But the satisfaction you get when you acquire or buy something new never really lasts. Sooner or later, you'll feel the emptiness and the dissatisfaction again. The feeling comes over you and you just have to buy another trinket to feel good. This can turn into a real problem as many people nowadays are struggling over how to make ends meet and pay their credit card bill, but they just can't seem to stop.

Escapism and Obsession with Celebrity

Another coping mechanism often employed by people around the globe is by distracting themselves from having to deal with problems in life. People would just rather disassociate themselves from reality through games, the internet, TV shows and even alcohol and other substances than face the problems in their lives. Because of this need for escape, it's getting easier and easier every day.

With the click of a button, you can actually live out a separate life, pretend to be someone else, or obsess over popular celebrities. But no matter how much you try to bury your problems in fantasy, reality will still be there waiting for you.

The Secret to Lasting Happiness

Meditation and mindfulness offers a different approach to the pursuit of happiness and the experience of life. It is a way of thought that has been developed and practiced since antiquity. It allows you to live with peace, happiness and love without the need for external gratification. Meditation and mindfulness cannot change any external factors that may affect your life, but they can have a huge effect on how you internally process these things.

The Answer is Internal

The problem with all the "solutions" that seem most available to everyone is that they don't really solve anything; they are simply ways for you to avoid dealing with negative emotions.

The simple point is that happiness doesn't equal material or external things. Happiness doesn't come by reaching an ideal, getting the right dress size, or earning a certain amount. So many wealthy, successful people still haven't figured out how to be happy. Similarly, there are people who barely have the essentials and still believe themselves to be quite happy. The secret behind happiness doesn't lie in what kind of life you have, but how you experience that life.

Meditation and mindfulness are able to give you a whole new perspective of acceptance and appreciation. Through meditation and mindfulness, you can learn to let go of all the perceptions in your mind that keep you from being happy and at peace.

Chapter 2: Techniques Used In Mindfulness Meditation

There are several techniques involved in mindfulness meditation and for specific purposes. Try and ask yourself what happens when you tell your mind to do something. Generally, what does happen is that your mind resists. For example, if you are lying in bed and want to sleep, it is often the thought of sleep which stops you from actually achieving it. Relaxation requires total immersion into the moment, rather than any kind of planning. If you tell yourself "I will sleep in a minute." chances are that you will still be awake in an hour because you are working your mind.

However, if you learn relaxation techniques that clear your mind, you are better able to sleep without having to try and reinforce the idea. Being present in the moment means that your mind will do the for you, rather than you having to work the mind. The Sudarshan kriya system of breathing will help you to do that. This is what is used as a tool to help you to achieve optimal results.

What has been discovered is that breathing in a certain rhythm helps the mind and breath to work together to form a very harmonious partnership. In every human body there is something which is called Prolactin. This is only released in any great quantity when you are feeling peaceful and happy.

If you practice this kind of breathing, you can find that you give your mind a great deal of powers and that your health improves as a direct result of using it. The heart and even the digestive system is improved by the breathing exercises, and you will find that any spiritual self realization can be achieved by learning the technique, which is detailed on an *online video*.

You will become more accustomed with the breathing exercises with practice, and these are used to make you feel a lot healthier and are also a way to train yourself to the discipline of meditation.

Other tools employed in mindfulness meditation include focusing on a certain point so that you are able to be taken away from your surroundings and submerse yourself in a kind of concentration that allows your mind to regenerate.

This is particularly useful in this stress filled world, as it not only allows the mind a rest, it allows it to become more powerful and focused once the meditation is performed. That's powerful stuff in the business world, and this system of meditation can be incorporated into your everyday life, to keep you tuned into the energy that you need to help you to make clear decisions and to enhance your chain of thought, so that nothing gets in the way of good decisions based on the "now" rather than being clouded by other thoughts.

Your mind is a very powerful tool and as you learn to use it and the breathing techniques involved in mindfulness, you will begin to see where Buddhist priests gain so much energy and are able to see things much more clearly than you are. Although you may never be in their position, you will be able to centralize your thoughts so that they are in that moment and embrace life as it unfolds.

Without incorporating these systems into your everyday life, you may struggle with emotional baggage, problems that fill your life with difficulty and not be able to see beyond those difficulties. The mind is too cluttered with information that doesn't need to be there and the tools of mindfulness meditation help you to clear the mind, so that it is better able to meet your needs.

Chapter 3: Coming Face To Face With Yourself

I find that the best introduction I can give students to mindfulness is to ask them to choose a place that inspires them. I would choose the top of a hill in beautiful countryside though others choose a beach at sunset or sunrise. The reason for this exercise is to introduce you to yourself. You need to have an acceptance of self in order to be able to practice mindfulness. Mindfulness doesn't mean having a mind full of something. It means being able to let go and be mindful of what's happening in this very time and space.

Self-acceptance is hard for a lot of people. They measure themselves by society standards. They may say things like "I am too fat," "I am not clever enough" or "I am not who my mother wants me to be" and there are a million other negative statements that people make to themselves every day of their lives. This exercise is to show you who you really are. Faced with the beauty of a site that you consider to be awesome, you begin to see how small human beings are in comparison to the world around them. It puts things back into perspective and helps you to learn what matters and what doesn't matter. Your shape, your intelligence, your ego are all things that don't matter at all. What matters is this acceptance of how small you are. It's called humility.

As you look around the scene that you have chosen as being something that inspires awe, you seem to be very close to something very special that some people call God. Others call it being close to their Creator. You don't have to be religious but an awesome sight can really pull you together in a very positive way. It makes you feel small in comparison and you need to strip yourself back to this smallness and then start to build on it. Instead of using negative statements to define who you are, you simply tell yourself that it isn't size that matters. If you were the equivalent to a grain of sand, what would a beach be like with no sand? Thus, you can see that smallness doesn't mean you have less importance. I feel that this exercise is necessary for anyone who is thinking of following the Mindfulness route because until you realize how small you are, how can you begin to build roots that will make you stronger and happier in yourself?

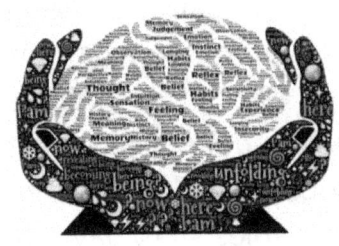

Chapter 4: About Mindfulness

When we first think of a mindful approach, we may not initially consider those students who are coming into their teenage years. We think of mindfulness as a resource for adults and an important tool for coping with life's problems. Mindfulness enables all to pay attention to thoughts, feelings and emotions. But these are not elements experienced by adults alone, children of all ages can be 'unmindful' and swayed by emotive responses or negative thoughts.

If you are teaching 11 to 16-year-olds, you will know first-hand that students are easily distracted by their peers or by their own thoughts. With so much learning to do, often students struggle to retain this information and lose motivation and focus. There is much evidence to suggest that a regular mindfulness practice would be beneficial to students of all ages but, in particular, those students who have a need for increased levels of concentration, empathy and impulse control. There is some thoughts that mindfulness, once grasped fully, enables adolescents to manage effectively the many challenges that lie ahead.

Teaching mindfulness may not always be easy, but planting the seed and explaining the many benefits attainable through regular practice will at least create solid foundations for the future and while some students may not be swayed by the benefits on offer, others will. As a teacher, you may well notice the development and progress of at least some of the students in your class as their understanding of mindfulness increases and as they embrace greater balance and wellbeing as a result.

The thought of slowing down, practicing breathing techniques, meditating regularly or even becoming disconnected from all the tempting digital devices that form part of everyday life may seem abhorrent but, it is possible to encourage a mindful approach by simply incorporating some of the techniques which aid greater focus.

Being mindful does not mean being judgemental or about succeeding or failing in thoughts or feelings.

Rather mindfulness is about balance in life and about embracing all that is here, right now. It's not about dreaming of tomorrow or ofthe years ahead, it's about creating the foundations for the future today. Each and every one of us is guilty of losing concentration from time to time, we start projects or adhere to tasks andour minds slip away unbidden. We don't stay in the moment for long and we fail to recognise when we slip into daydreams.

The same happens with the students at school, at home and, later on, in the workplace.

Thoughts and feelings can distract us, noisy chatter from a group of students can distract others who may have a more diligent approach, but even the most dedicated of students will not be fully engaged at all times. So mindfulness helps the students to return their focus to the lesson in a gentle but firm manner.

The best way to emphasise the many benefits of regular mindfulness practice is to live it yourself. This is why we advocate you as the teacher, working your way through this training programme trying out some of the tasks and applying them to your everyday life. By doing so, you will understand the ethos of mindfulness and will gain the benefits yourself which will make it much easier to be able to extend your personal experiences to others. Everyone around you will notice a differencein only a short time. You'll seem calmer, more purposeful, more decisive and patient.

The changes of mindfulness are noticeable.

Teachers are often under a great deal of stress in their place of work and without a doubt, students will pick up on the tension emitted when you are under pressure. Equally, through mindfulness, students will start to notice a calmer vibe as you start to increase your own productivity, reduce stress and anxiety and be able to enjoy life in its simplest format. This means that the most productive way to ensure your students begin to take mindfulness seriously, is to let them see it in action.

People often have very definite ideas about mindfulness and what it means in general. They want to know how it can benefit them on a personal level.

Selling the benefits is important and they need to be able to calculate how it can improve their life in the present not simply by saying how good their lives will be in the future. Time has little meaning to a student. They also live busy lives, while improving their ability to be productive is a skill worth having, this will not seem much like a personal benefit.

Research has indicated that:
☐ Mindfulness can improve concentration
☐ Mindfulness can reduce feeligs of anxiety, stress and even depression.

You may find that your students are fascinated by the prospect of mindfulness being a type of training for their mind-sets. If you know your students really well, you will be able to list the type of benefits on an individual level, for example, a student who is prone to emotional responses and who often gets themselves in trouble as a result may feel that mindfulness can help them to control this raw reaction. A student who can never make up their mind about anything, may find that mindfulness will empower their decision-making skills. In fact, mindfulness also plays a definite role in the neuroplasticity of the brain.

Students may not contemplate a positive awareness of mindfulness initially, but once they understand the basics and try it out, the results are quick to follow. Even if they do not admit it, students get anxious about a lot of things. Thoughts are jumbled, they have self-doubts, selflimitations, self-esteem issues as well as needing to cope with fluctuating emotions and, still learn all the school syllabus. Mindfulness helps them to alleviate high stress levels, it brings balance back to an unbalanced life, and it also increases calmness and well-being. So mindfulness can help prevent a series of negative thoughts which can actually restricts the individual's progress in life such as:

☐ I don't understand math and I'm never going to understand it. I must be stupid.
☐ I'm studying like mad but I can't seem to learn enough. I'm going to fail my exams.
☐ I'm never going to get into college.

When you teach mindfulness, you can explain how much of mental chatter occurs. They may experience a constant stream of thoughts that can work against them and not for them. It's important to note that these thoughts are just that, they are thoughts and not real.

Feelings of anxiety project inner angst and this increases emotional and even physical stress. Mindfulness teaches students to become aware of their thoughts and to judge them as worrying thoughts rather than their becoming embroiled in the negativity.

The benefits of mindfulness are far-reaching and with regular practice and commitment, it can gradually infiltrate every part of life improving:
- [ ] Confidence
- [ ] Balance in life
- [ ] Self-esteem
- [ ] Positive thoughts and feelings
- [ ] Health
- [ ] Learning
- [ ] Adapting
- [ ] Focus

So students will discover that the many benefits also extend to their personal lives too.

You will find that some students have a very natural curiosity about mindfulness and will start to embrace the tasks and the experiences, and will naturally start to apply some of the techniques into their lives afterwards. Others may not respond as well but, by planting the seed and by bringing awareness of the subject, it may be something that they move towards in due course.

Task:

Ask the students what mindfulness means to them. It is likely that they will have heard the term but an interactive class discussion will foster a safe environment for the positive seed of mindfulness to grow.

Chapter 5: What Is Mindfulness Meditation?

One of the major techniques used by Buddhists monks and the one which is highly popular in the western part of the globe is *mindfulness meditation.*

Mindfulness meditation is practiced by first allowing the thoughts to pass through as it flows and then watching as to what kind of thoughts are cropping up while staying disconnected from the thoughts. The mind is a mad monkey and it is quite impractical to try and stop your thoughts all of a sudden.

Why do we need to stop our thoughts at all? The mind is a tool. We stop the running thoughts in order to gain control over our mind and make it act as we wish. When we reach this stage, we would be able to achieve the impossible. That's the main aim of mindfulness meditation.

Mindfulness meditation is also associated with breathing techniques. Normal people might just think of breathing as just a feeling, but there is much more to it. When it comes to controlling the breath, it is an art by itself and that's part of the foundation of mindfulness meditation. It is been proven by many studies that by varying your breathing model it is possible to alter your body's entire energy level.

Mind is represented by the "I" aspect innate in us. It is that entity which reveals itself as the ego in man or woman. If this ego is cut down by control of mind, only the supreme truth will shine. I know that sounds kind of out there, but when you break it down, mindfulness meditation brings about truth in our lives; truth in the moment. This state can be achieved by constant practice of mindfulness meditation wherein at one point the thoughtlessness stage is attained and the mind is under control.

The vitality of controlling your breath lies in cutting even the slightest ego factor in us, to show the real true self inside of us.

So, when we can control breath, we can control our mind.

However, what we need to take into account is that breath control can only subdue the mind temporarily. Techniques and practices like pranayama (breath control), repeating a deity's name several times (Japa) or chanting a mantra are all different methods to control our minds. But only with deeper mindfulness meditation techniques we can quiet the mind; we can reach a thoughtlessness stage. Mindfulness meditation is the primary technique that can help us achieve this state.

WHAT IS NEUROPLASTICITY?

To put it in simple terms, neuroplasticity is the process by which our brain redesigns itself in order to fulfill a desired result. Our nervous system is capable of reorganizing its structure according to various experiences and impacts created externally and internally. As a result of practicing particular neural pathways constantly, the mind can change itself physically in order to fulfill mental processes.

Here's a way to think about it: Imagine you grew up in the woods. Every day you took the same few paths to get the things you needed to sustain yourself; you never strayed from those paths at all. Then one day as you walk down your normal path, that is heavily worn from years of use, down to the river; you notice a little building way off the trail you're on. You think, *wow I'd like to check that out*, but you've never been off the trail. You decide to go check it out. You leave the worn path that you were on to step onto ground that you've never stepped foot on before. You approach the door of the building, then walk inside to notice that there is a large volume of books on the subject of building log cabins. You are looking around the room and notice a note on a table that states you are welcome to use the place anytime you want, but you're never to take the books from the building with you.

So you begin to come and go every day to read and focus on learning how to build new log cabins. Every day as you come and go you begin to develop two fresh paths that diverge off of the worn river path that you use to get to the building. When walking to the cabin everyday these fresh paths begin to become worn and easily noticeable. Even though the paths never become as ingrained and worn as your original paths they are still distinct and worn. This is similar to how neuroplasticity occurs in our brains as we learn something new. The more we repeat something and use that portion of the brain in a focused way new neural pathways might develop in your brain.

Chapter 6: Postures To Practice Mindfulness

As a beginner you should pick one posture at a time that you feel is suitable for you. Once you have some experience and have developed your skills then you may want to try other postures. Below are postures that you may want to choose from.

Reclining Posture.

This is also referred to as the 'lion posture'. With this posture you lie down on your left side, resting your head on your right hand, and extending your left arm resting it on top of your body.

Standing Posture.

In this posture you may want to lift your arms with your palms facing you. Your feet should be about shoulder width apart and do not lock your knees. Also try and relax your stomach and lower back.

Walking Posture.

This is a great way to do Mindfulness meditation over and over again. It will be the easiest one to fit into your daily life schedule. It is best to do it in a secluded area with the least distractions. You can focus on the intention of moving as you are taking each step to walk, or on other parts of your body.

Seated Posture.

This is a posture that would be very easy to maintain as a beginner. You will be able to practice your Mindfulness in a comfortable sitting position. You may choose to fold your legs into half a lotus, this is one leg folded unto other leg. The full lotus is both legs folded unto each other. You may want your palms facing upward with index fingers gently touching thumb. Your chest should be upright and open, and your stomach and lower back should be relaxed. Some have their soles of feet touching while toes point away from the body. You may rest your hands on your thighs, or folded gently in your lap. To make sure that your airways are open your head should be gently tilted forward with your neck balanced.

Chapter 7: Defining Mindfulness

Observe the body and mind to cultivate Self-Awareness

Body Awareness

Take a moment to think about the reality of Stress, Anxiety, and Fear. These feelings are the names we have given to uncomfortable bodily states that come about in response to certain stimuli. This is why you cannot talk yourself out of a particular mood. No matter what is said, the physical state remains; our nerves are transmitting the same sensations to our brains. The thoughts and matters that trigger these feelings are as varied as the people who experience them. Though they share a common origin in the biological defense mechanisms that aid in our survival.

Imagine yourself happening upon a Tiger in the wild. Your body would react faster than you can think– increasing your pulse, narrowing your senses, and strengthening the blood flow to your vital organs and muscles, readying you for action. This reaction is known as the Fight or Flight Response and it prepares us to answer a perceived danger in the most effective way possible. This response is instrumental to keeping us alive in the face of danger. But our physiology has yet to catch up with the dynamism of our minds.

Our brains cannot tell the difference between a real, external threat and one contrived by the process of destructive thinking. Thus the same bodily stress responses that we experience in dangerous matters are also triggered by negative thoughts. Regardless of if the perceived threat is something that can actually harm us.

Therefore when we experience some matter that we think is stressful, consider a matter that we think brings us anxiety, or dwell on something that we think we fear, we trigger the same regions of the brain that activate in response to real danger. Your brain sees no distinction between the attacks of an outside aggressor and attacks manufactured by your internal monologue.

Think about the last time you were stressed, anxious or afraid. It's more than just a state of mind, isn't it? There is a certain, identifiable tension that occurs throughout the body. And it is in recognizing this tension and naming it accordingly that the conscious experience of Stress, Anxiety and Fear are created. This activates a negative feedback loop in which believing that a matter is stressful causes tension, we feel the tension that arises from this belief and think that we are in distress, which just causes the brain to keep us tense, which results in further thoughts that we are stressed. This is why these negative experiences last far longer than whatever triggers them.

Developing Body Awareness is key to living mindfully. You will cultivate your Self-Awareness to the point that you can recognize where the tension is in your body. Once found you will be able to neutralize this tension, letting it go to consciously relax your muscles, and free yourself from the negative feedback loop. The benefits that this will bring to your health are profound.

Mind Awareness

Rumination is dwelling on depressive thoughts. This serves as the fuel of any stressful cycle. After the initial stimuli that triggers any negative episode, it is rumination that keeps it in the mind and body. This process is a result of a mechanism in our brains that attempts to make sense of the bodily tensions and tries to figure out the reason behind the triggering matter.

What just happened?

Why did it happen?

How do I feel about it?

Why do I feel this way?

Our minds fixate on examining the matter – rationalizing all available variables of the situation to determine a conscious narrative that explains our mental state. This is an automatic pattern which works well when applied to positive events. We craft a line of reasoning for why we are feeling well or in good spirits. It also helps us put together the important details needed to deal with external challenges. But when it comes to the internal pressures that ail us at times, the rumination that follows can be endless.

Unlike external dangers that can be escaped or dealt with, the internal threats -- of which our brains see no distinction -- stick with us for as long as we are thinking about them. When we concentrate on a bad situation an avalanche of stressed and anxious thoughts follow. Thus, one matter or circumstance steadily grows in our minds to an enormous problem and produces an accompanying stress response that is not proportional with its reality. This is often coupled with our tendency to revisit traumas from the past to identify the pattern, and imagine future stressful matters to show us what to avoid. We find ourselves on a downward spiral of negativity, somehow worse off than where we began.

By increasing voluntary control and awareness of the mind, Mindfulness greatly decreases rumination. Through Mindfulness, it is much easier to pick up on depressive thoughts and disarm them before they get out of control. Instead of getting into the mindset of trying to dissect or deny the trigger and its assumed emotional consequences, we look at it mindfully and see it as it actually is.

What does it mean to see something as it actually is? Imagine you are out driving your car one day and you get a flat tire. This happens to many people daily, annoying them to no end. You see your flat tire and then you start thinking about how late you are going to be, how much a repair will cost, or how unexpected and unwanted this entire ordeal is. Suddenly you feel your blood pumping and your skin heating in rage. You expend all of that energy and your problem is not one step closer to being resolved.

What just happened here? Well you might say that getting a flat tire made you upset. But being Mindful is looking at the flat tire and realizing that a hole in a rubber tube made the air within it escape. And there is nothing intrinsically or immediately threatening to your wellbeing about that happening. Mindfulness is the awareness of the reality of the matters in life and most importantly **your choice** in how you want to react to them.

Most of our reactions are automatic and deeply ingrained in our habits. These habits are learned from watching how others respond to certain events, off of which we model our own behavior. By being aware of the reality of situations and actively -— instead of reactively -- choosing the thoughts that we think about them, we gain control over our mind and circumstances instead of letting them control us. With time and practice this becomes second nature. Mindfulness is freedom from the unproductive analyses and judgements of the world around us. Opening us to experience and acknowledge the full picture. We get out of our heads and take in the world with all of our senses.

Acceptance

The prolific product of Self Awareness is Acceptance. To live in the moment is to accept the present experience. We are constantly evaluating our thinking: placing each thought between the poles of good and bad, trying to determine its efficacy and use. Mindfulness allows us to observe our thoughts without judging them, accepting the thoughts occurring in our minds as exactly what they are – subjective and symbolic representations of the world. By understanding the nature of thought, we are come to understand and accept the world too.

Cognitive dissonance is the negative stress that occurs when holds conflicting beliefs. The aforementioned burdens are each a form of this phenomenon, in which our belief of what is happening does not match our belief of what should be. The key here is that when we choose to let something get us angry, stressed, anxious, or depressed, these feelings take root as a direct result of us simply thinking that they are there. The Mindful know not to over-identify with the erratic expressions of the mind, for we are aware of its ever-changing state. Through acceptance we no longer need to cling. Everything is in motion; all things come and go.

Take notice of your initial reactions and identify your habits. Acknowledging our patterns of behavior can help us refrain from unnecessary reactions in the future and reduce the amount of stress we experience immeasurably. The outcome of thought observation is acceptance. We observe the thoughts in our mind and accept the events in our world. Seeing everything as it is first opens us to making proper judgements and wiser decisions.

Chapter 8: What Is Mindfulness?

Anxiety is a life-limiting state of being. It can affect every area of your life, from relationships, to sleep and job success. Being constantly impacted by anxiety can feel crushing, with sufferers feeling they are at the mercy of their emotions.

However, there is a way out. By using mindfulness meditation, you can learn how to befriend your anxiety and gain greater control over it.

Mindfulness has been steadily gaining popularity amongst health professionals and members of the public over the last decade. Many people have now learned for themselves about the powerful benefits that mindfulness practice can bring.

For those who have never heard of it or don't know how to practice, it may seem confusing and difficult to know where to start. This book will guide you through the basics of mindfulness, and through a series of exercises, show you how you can incorporate it into your life, for a healthier and more relaxed you.

What is Mindfulness?

Many people have a certain picture in their head when it comes to mindfulness and meditation in general. This picture may involve someone sitting on a cushion with his or her legs crossed, spending hours sitting still and going into a trancelike state. The picture evolves to include the person floating into a place of no thoughts, the mind completely quiet.

It's unfortunate this picture persists for many, because nothing could be farther from the truth.

Rather than having no thoughts or entering a state where you are unaware of your surroundings, mindfulness teaches us the exact opposite. It is a practice that enables you to get to know yourself intimately, and to feel in more detail what is happening in your body and mind.

Definition of Mindfulness:

Mindfulness is a way of paying attention to our thoughts and physical sensations, but one that teaches us not to attach to them too rigidly. The process of doing this helps us to accept and embrace our whole being. Mindfulness is a gentle invitation to become more aware of who we are, and learn to accept ourselves more, without trying to judge or change what is happening in each moment.

For those who have never practiced mindfulness, it can be an incredibly liberating and powerful experience.

Far from having to sit still for hours on end, mindfulness is also something which people are encouraged to practice while taking part in activities such as mindful yoga, or mindful walking. You can also incorporate it into your everyday activities - even doing your dishes or taking a shower can be something you do mindfully.

What are the benefits of Mindfulness?

There have been many studies in recent years into mindfulness and the effects it has on both the brain and the reported experiences of those who have practiced.

During one study in which participants took an eight-week course in mindfulness, differences were discovered in the amygdala. Magnetic Resonance Imaging or 'MRI' scans showed that the amygdala – which is the area of the brain that houses our primal 'fight or flight' center - began to shrink. In addition, another area of the brain – the pre-frontal cortex – got thicker. The amygdala governs emotions like stress and fear, and the prefrontal cortex is responsible for decision-making, concentration and awareness.

The study also showed a lessening of the area that sends off 'danger' signals, and a thickening of the area that helps to process information and heighten concentration. The way these two regions interacted with each other also changed. Connections between the fear-response center and the rest of the brain got weaker, while connections from the prefrontal cortex got stronger. This shows us that mindfulness has very real and has profound effects on the way our minds function.

Other studies have shown that mindfulness is also effective at helping people cope with physical pain. Advanced practitioners in mindfulness reported feeling pain on a less intense level than those who do not practice. What is remarkable is that MRI scans showed that their brains were not actually registering *less* pain. It appears as though what happened was the mindfulness practitioner was able to change their *relationship* to pain, by lessening strong sensations of aversion.

Self-efficacy is another aspect of our lives that mindfulness can help with. Self-efficacy is the level at which a person feels they can exercise control and acceptance over their emotions and life events. Because mindfulness practitioners have become experienced in allowing and accepting their circumstances without self-judgment, they felt calmer and more in control. It might seem like a contradiction that accepting something means you can change it, but this is exactly how mindfulness works.

There is a saying common among people who practice mindfulness –

"What we resist, persists."

When you have learned to let go of the fight against your body and mind (including trying to shut out sensations completely), you are then free to allow it to move on.

This concept may seem challenging when you begin to learn, but over time you will begin to see amazing benefits.

Chapter 9: Using Mindfulness To Become Happier, Peaceful, And Focused

In addition to curing conditions related to depression, anxiety, and stress, mindfulness can also infuse happiness and peace in your life. It can cure your physical conditions and enhance your emotional, mental, and physical well-being by manifolds. Here is how:

How Mindfulness helps you Become Happier, Peaceful, and Focused

In terms of affecting happiness, focus, and peace in your life, mindfulness has the following positive effects.

Mindfulness Alters Gene Activity

Dr. Bruce Lipton, a renowned developmental biologist, best recognized for publicizing the notion that your beliefs can manipulate your DNA and genes, states that the gene activity occurring in your body changes daily.

If your perception reflects on your body's chemistry and your nervous system can read and interpret everything in the environment, as well as control your blood's chemistry and structure, it is logical to conclude that you can actually alter the destiny of cells in your body by changing your thoughts.

Dr. Lipton's work clearly illustrates that if you positively alter your perception, you will be capable of changing how your genes behave. This control effectively enables you to bring changes to the numerous variations your genes bring into your body on a daily basis. This in turn means that if you can change your thinking pattern, you can make your genes behave how you want them to, and prevent them from bringing disastrous changes such as tumors and cancer in your body.

Moreover, you can use your thoughts to effect the 'nocebo effect' that often takes place in your body when you are diagnosed with a deadly disease, or receive news of your impending death. The nocebo effect causes you to pay heed to negative thoughts that make you believe in your impending death.

By learning how to control your thoughts, you can easily neutralize the nocebo effect, thus increasing your lifespan, as well as gaining complete peace of mind. Dr. Lipton also states that the best way to gain mastery of your thoughts is through mindfulness. Therefore, if you want to enjoy a full life, try mindfulness.

Mindfulness Techniques for Happiness and Complete Well-being

We have discussed Mindfulness based meditation in a previous chapter. If you continue with that, you can slowly gain control over your thoughts and use them to your advantage.

We shall not go back to that. Instead, in this bit, we shall discuss a few more mindfulness techniques (so you have a variety of exercises to try, and choose from). The idea is to infuse mindfulness in every aspect of your life, so that whatever you do and wherever you are doing it, you are fully alert, conscious, and aware of every tiny thing happening inside and outside you. The more mindful you are, the easier it will be to disconnect from negative thinking and worrying, and enjoy the present.

Mindful Immersion

Mindful immersion helps you to become fully engrossed in the present moment. It helps cultivate full contentment in your present, so you can escape the constant striving you routinely become caught up in.

If you observe yourself while performing routine chores, you will realize that you anxiously want to complete one daily chore so that you can move on to another. This makes you impatient. You are always in a hurry and are never able to get deeply involved in one chore at a time and enjoy its completion.

You start working like a robot whose sole job is to get things done on time. This routine makes things annoying and tiring for you. To escape this monotony and exhaustion, practice mindfulness immersion to help you find relief from the habit of worrying about things 24/7.

How to Practice Mindfulness Immersion

To practice mindfulness immersion, get started on a routine chore. For instance, if you start cleaning your room, do it in detail, and pay complete attention to every minute detail of this task.

Do not treat it as a routine chore. Rather, change it into a new experience by observing every little aspect of the actions you perform as you perform the task. If you are sweeping the floor, become involved in the sweeping motion and feel the movement of the broom as you move it. Sense the muscles that become involved in this act.

The more engrossed you become in this simple chore, the more relaxed you will feel. You will find the pressure of working like a robot slowly sliding off your mind and body. Moreover, you will become creative with the practice and maybe come up with an exciting new way of sweeping the floor.

Similarly, try this technique with every routine chore you engage it, be it reading a book, cooking, or making your bed. This simple practice, if adopted for good, can help you become calm, serene, and happy and when this happens, you can easily control your thoughts and influence them.

Mindful Appreciation

Mindfulness appreciation is a simple, but truly effective practice that helps you become more cognizant and appreciative of the gifts you have in your life. By recognizing your blessings, you become thankful of things you have and start becoming peaceful with loses. When the grief associated with losing things and people starts diminishing, your mind, and thoughts start grounding in the present.

Here's how you can practice mindful appreciation.

How to Practice Mindfulness Appreciation

To practice mindfulness appreciation, start by noticing any five things that normally go unnoticed and unappreciated; these five things can be people or objects. Make a daily practice of noticing five new things and jot them down in your journal. When the day ends, understand the importance of these five things in your life, appreciate them, and express your gratitude for them.

These things support your existence and are important to a healthy living, but since you are always striving for bigger, better, and more luxurious things and lifestyle, you fail to recognize these important things.

Your list of things could include; electricity, water, air, house, pots, and pans, your postal worker, your plumber, your organs, your body, your five senses, your parents, your siblings, and several other important things and people similar to these.

After identifying the five things, dig deeper into them and find out how they came into being, what benefits they provide you, and how difficult your life can become without those things. This will help you truly understand their significance and be thankful for them. Make sure to practice this exercise daily, so that you can appreciate your life more and start living it fully.

Mindful Awareness

Mindful awareness is an exercise that cultivates heightened appreciation and awareness of the simple chores you perform daily, and the results you achieve with them. The aim of this practice, like all the other mindfulness-based exercises, is to ground you in the present so that you can control your thoughts and make them live in the now and not the past or future.

Here's how you can integrate this exercise into your life.

How to Practice Mindfulness Awareness

Think of an activity that takes place several times a day. The activity could be as simple as opening a door, holding your laptop, or drinking water. Next, when you engage in that specific activity, become more mindful of it.

For instance, if you are opening the door, become mindful and alert of where you're standing, the doorknob you are touching and how you are feeling. Appreciate the fact that this door leads to somewhere and gives you an exit point.

Apply this technique to your thinking pattern. Every time a negative thought enters your mind, pause for a moment, think of a suitable label for it, such as unhelpful or unhealthy, and then release it. Whenever a positive thought enters your mind, label it too, and then appreciate it. By doing this, you will be appreciating, and becoming aware of what you have, and will be releasing negativity from your mind as soon it enters it.

Practice these three mindfulness exercises to enhance your well-being and achieve a state of blissful happiness.

Chapter 10: Mindfulness Defined

What do you think of when you hear the word "mindfulness?" For most people who haven't heard much about mindfulness before, it simply means using your mind. It's more than that, though. It's about paying attention and a particular type of attention at that. You can practice mindfulness at a specific time and place or you can practice it wherever and whenever you like. But before you start learning how to practice mindfulness, it's important to know exactly what it is.

Being Fully Present Here and Now

You've probably heard people say "carpe diem" or "seize the day." Phrases like this can seem idealistic. Of course, you want to take opportunities that come to you, of course you do! But sometimes, life seems to get in the way. Instead of being fully present in each moment, right where you are, it seems more important to think of what you need to do next. And, you find yourself wondering about how the things you've just done and said are going to affect the future.

Yet, it really is true that this one moment is all you really have. How can that be? Don't you have memories of the past and plans for the future? You almost certainly do. But here's the thing to remember: those images, thoughts, ideas and plans can be a part of this precious moment. That is, they can as long as you direct your focus to what you have power to do and be in this given moment.

Can you brainstorm right now to come up with solutions to problems? Can you share a memory with a loved one or create something that expresses your thoughts and feelings from the past? Can you make concrete plans or begin preparations for the future? Can you, in fact, do anything about these issues other than mull them over? If so, you can practice mindfulness about these things. If not, you're focused squarely on something you can't change.

Noticing What's Going On around You

Most people in developed countries tend to spend a lot of time living inside their heads. Have you ever spaced out while going somewhere in your car? When that happens, you can be aware of your surroundings one minute and lost in your thoughts the next. Sometimes, you can go for many miles, driving on virtual autopilot, until you wake up to your surroundings many miles later. You may be stuck inside your mind, but you aren't practicing mindfulness.

Now, think about those eyewitnesses who can't agree on a clear description of a criminal. They all believe they know what happened and what the person looked like. What actually happens most often is that they are walking around, unaware of their surroundings, until something catches their attention. Then, at that crucial moment, they're so startled by it they have trouble registering the details of the person and event in their minds. Their minds were just too full of things that don't relate to the moment.

If you were being mindful when a crime took place, most likely you'd see the signs that something was about to happen. You'd be prepared for it when it happened so you could capture the details in your mind at the critical moment. You might even be able to respond better to the crisis, whether to help, protect yourself and your loved ones, or report the crime accurately.

This ability to notice your surroundings doesn't mean you have to be suspicious of every situation, either. Unwarranted suspicion isn't mindfulness at all. Once again, you're paying more attention to your imagination than you are to the event that is unfolding. On the other hand, if you are mindfully aware, you notice these things only as they're actually happening.

Being Non-Judgmentally Aware

There's nothing at all wrong with exercising discretion as you live your life. In fact, it's the healthiest and most successful way to make decisions. You see your own version of the pluses and minuses of any situation and make a decision based on what seems right to and for you.

Judgment is different. When you judge, you aren't thinking of what you need to do or not do. Instead, you're looking at the situation or person with the purposes of identifying the objective truth and making decisions based on a set standard. There is a place for judgment. If not, why would citizens elect judges or allow taxes to be collected to pay for their services?

Judges have an important place in civilized society. But their judgements are (or should) come from outside the situation. That's the main reason judges or lawyers sometimes recuse themselves – to avoid a conflict of interest. When you exercise discretion, you are right in the thick of things. You are experiencing the situation yourself and deciding what to do about it based on your own standards.

So, how does this relate to mindfulness, you might ask. The answer is simple. As you go about your daily life, situations will present themselves that will require you to exercise discretion. But, unless you're an appointed judge, you have no reason to pronounce judgment. It serves no purpose for you. It clouds your mind with unnecessary thoughts.

Releasing Obsessive Thoughts

To be mindful, you need to suspend judgment, not only of people and events, but also of the thoughts that cross your mind – even if they're judgments! Your thoughts aren't bad or good, they just are. But, here's something to think about: not all thoughts are important. Not all thoughts relate to reality.

You might have trouble accepting the fact that your thoughts aren't necessarily valuable. You have a lot of motivation for dwelling on specific thoughts. Maybe you felt clever when you come up with the thought. Perhaps the thought validates an argument you've built up in your mind. Or, maybe the thought helps you justify feeling miserable. In each of these cases, the thought is worth noticing, but it doesn't help you to keep replaying the thought over and over.

You might not even be aware of how obsessive your thoughts can be. As you rehash past disappointments, failures or hurts, you might feel like it's an important activity, as if it's making you feel better and stronger. But, it is really making you feel that way? If you're honest, your answer will be no in most cases. So, let go of replaying old memories for the sake of convincing yourself how right you were or how wronged you were. As you let your thoughts flow freely without holding onto them, you become more mindful of the present moment.

Sharpening Your Focus

Mindfulness, as a practice of embracing the present moment, can only happen if you're sharply focused on the present. If you're eating, you're paying attention to the details of the meal, the sensations you feel and the way you deal with the food by eating it and enjoying it. This requires a deep level of concentration, which you'll develop more strongly as you continue to practice mindfulness.

Letting New Insights Come

When you're truly mindful, your brain isn't weighed down by unnecessary thoughts. As you develop the skill of mindfulness, you'll begin to achieve more and more moments of clarity and insight. You can't make these moments happen by willing them directly. You can't say to yourself that today you'll have an insight into this or that issue. What you can do is say that today you'll practice mindfulness and appreciate any ah-ha moments that arise.

Chapter 11: What Is Mindfulness?

We all exist in two vastly different worlds at the same time. We have the external world that's made up of all the things we can experience with our five physical senses. And then we have the internal world, the personal world, where we experience our thoughts, emotions and whatever belief systems govern our decisions on a moment-to-moment basis.

As important as the external world is, what exists within us is of immeasurable value. It is our personal world 'view', if you will, that ultimately shapes our perception of the external reality. What one person experiences as a tree standing in a park could be something entirely different to someone else, with the difference based on what's going on internally for each person.

During every moment of our lives, there are internal processes prompting us to do whatever it is that we find ourselves doing in that moment. Let's take the present, for example. Right now you're reading these words, perhaps in your bedroom, maybe on a long-haul flight, or even on a beach in the Bahamas. But something called you to read this, something internal. Sure, you may have seen the name pop up on the side of the screen or you possibly searched for the word 'mindfulness'. Irrespective of what external forces brought you to this moment where you find yourself reading this book, you're still here because something inside of you called you to embark on this journey to mindfulness.

That internal process, whether conscious or unconscious, is something we're all familiar with. Yet so many of us don't pay attention to it. We simply follow that intuitive voice without a second thought. And this is where mindfulness comes in – by allowing you to become fully aware and thus able to play an active role in any and all internal processes that determine your experience of the external world.

It is t he process of creation itself.

Understanding the mind The mind: the seat of thoughts, imagination, processes, judgements, dreams and decisions. It is the mind that analyses – consciously or subconsciously – every situation and enables us to determine what to think and how to react in any given scenario. Subconsciously, the mind is able to direct our bodily functions to prevent a fall. Consciously, the mind has the power to shape what we experience in reality.

And the way the mind makes decisions on a conscious and subconscious level is different for every single person in every single situation. It's very rare to have two people react to or perceive something in exactly the same way. For example, person A walks into a room full of strangers and thinks: "Wow, I don't know a single person here. What an incredible opportunity to meet new friends." Person B, however, might say: "Oh no, I don't know anyone here. I'll just go home."

Through this example, it's clear that every individual's perception of a situation will shape the experience of it. The same principle applies to everything we do on a daily basis. When you wake up in the morning with little energy for the day, thinking about how lovely it would be to stay in bed and not face the tasks at hand, your mindset is creating the environment for the rest of the day. You'll start to feel even more sluggish as you drag yourself out from under the comfort of your blankets, and you'll more than likely have unpleasant or negative experiences throughout the day as you now perceive everything as somewhat of an inconvenience.

However, rising in the morning with grateful and positive thoughts – such as "Wow, I'm alive. I've never been in this time and space before. Anything can happen today and I'm so excited to experience the magic that this day may bring." – will set the tone for the rest of your day. With a positive mindset, everything good or bad that happens to you and around you will naturally be perceived as a new experience from which to grow and learn.

This mindset, when harnessed correctly and activated on a daily basis, will help you to create a life of excitement, joy, openness, creativity and love. We need no further proof to know that our minds play an all-important role in shaping our experience of both the internal and external worlds we experience. And the most exciting part is that we own the power to make choices that can positively alter the way our minds work, ultimately changing our own reality.

Chapter 12: Understanding Mindfulness

Before we dig deeper into this topic, it will be appropriate to let you in on what mindfulness is and what it means to live mindfully.

By definition, mindfulness is a state of maximum concentration and focus on what you are presently engaged in without allowing anything, past or future, to invade your mind and break your concentration. When you live mindfully, you learn to take life one step at a time, refuse to live in the past or worry about what the future might possibly hold; you simply enjoy each moment as it passes.

Mindfulness helps you achieve more centeredness and balance in life. A mindful life helps you become more appreciative of the things you have going for you. Mindful living also helps you recognize your strengths and take advantage of them. When you focus on your strengths, you stop focusing on your weaknesses and faults.

Mindful living helps you appreciate all the important things life offers you freely, things you have hitherto overlooked or taken for granted. For instance, the air you breathe comes without a price tag. The life you live is a free one; so is the rain, the breeze, the sunshine, the melodious rhythm of singing birds in the garden, the calming scent of roses, the soothing scent of most natural fragrances, and several other free gifts of nature. When you start being mindful, you become more aware and appreciative of such minute things.

Mindful living helps you take note of the sensation you experience as you inhale and exhale during breathing. It ensures you savor the aroma and taste of your most cherished delicacies, and relish the sweetness of a cold/warm bath. It gives you a deeper sense of gratitude for being alive with food on your table, a roof over your head, a beautiful family, the amazing friends that make your life more meaningful and enjoyable, the monthly paycheck that helps you pay the bills, and all other blessings several people are wishing to have in their own lives.

The result of a mindful life is a life devoid of every trace of worry, anxiety, and every other thing that contributes to increased stress levels. As we move further in this book, we will look at some of the scientifically proven benefits of mindfulness and certain techniques that when practiced for at least 5 minutes daily, will help you win the battle against stress and anxiety.

Chapter 13: Mindfulness

It's a busy, fast-paced world we live in. Every single day, people are doing their best to keep up with everything that they need to do - from the simple task of folding the laundry and preparing food for their children, to finishing work that should have been done the day before. There is always a frantic rush to do every single thing and it is because of this that people often lose touch with the present moment, often doing things without fully absorbing it.

Whenever this happens, we end up losing touch with ourselves, too. Have you ever paused for a moment and thought about how you're feeling? Do you feel well-rested or are you so overwhelmed that you feel absolutely nothing at all?

So What is Mindfulness?

This is the act of focusing your attention on the present moment, doing it with intent and accepting this state of mind without any judgment. It may seem like such a small thing, but scientific studies have shown that it is one of the key elements for achieving happiness as well as peace of mind.

Mindfulness can trace its roots back to Buddhism. However, many religions have always included a form of meditation technique, which helps individuals shift their thoughts to the present moment. This allows the person to focus on what is happening right now and what needs to be done instead of worrying about the things that have come to pass as well as those that have yet to. Just about everyone is guilty of this, spending too much time pondering on things that they have no control over instead of working on those that they have the power to change.

There's been plenty of research done regarding the benefits of mindfulness and the results have been promising. In fact, this is one of the reasons as to why the practice is being introduced into mainstream medicine. Clinical studies show that mindfulness meditation can help bring about significant improvements when it comes to the physical as well as psychological symptoms a person may be experiencing. Aside from this, it can also help create positive changes in their behaviour and attitude, enabling people to develop healthier lifestyles and habits.

Mindfulness and Our Physical Health

One of the things you'll learn upon practicing mindfulness will be the fact that everything about our self is connected. This includes the physical, mental and spiritual self - all of which affect the other in varying ways. For example, mental stress can eventually cause us to feel lethargic and in some cases, we end up falling ill because of it. A sick body isn't all that great for our spirituality as well.

Fortunately, mindfulness benefits the physical body too. It can:

Help in relieving tension in the body, allowing it to better relax. Too much adrenaline can actually damage the immune system, do take note of this.

Help lower risks of heart disease. This is connected to stress, of course, and how it can put too much strain on our body - particularly, the heart.

Lower blood pressure. Stress, anxiety, exhaustion - these are just some of the things that can cause our blood pressure to rise. This is very risky, of course, and it is important that we're able to keep it in check.

There are many different types of chronic pain, but its effect on the body is more or less the same. It can completely paralyze a person and prevent them from doing something that they enjoy. In time, it can also take a mental toll on the person experiencing it. Mindfulness can help alleviate its symptoms and change the way people view their illness. A change in one's mindset can significantly alter the way he experiences things, after all.

It can also help improve the quality of sleep that you get. The better rested you are, the better you function both mentally and physically. You're able to think faster on your feet and you'll have more energy at your disposal throughout the day.

Mindfulness and Mental Health:

Mindfulness has also been found to have uses and benefits when it comes to helping us maintain mental health. In recent years, a significant number of psychotherapists have implemented the use of mindfulness meditation when it comes to treating different mental health problems such as:

Substance abuse

Depression

Conflicts between couples and siblings

Anxiety disorders

Obsessive compulsive disorder

How does it help? Experts believe that mindfulness works by enabling people to better the things they experience, including the more painful emotions that they tend to avoid or deny completely in order to not feel anything. Mindfulness also teaches people how to have better control over their reactions and gain better perspective when it comes to challenging situations that can take a mental toll on them.

On the topic of mental health treatments, it has become increasingly common for psychotherapists to combine mindfulness meditation with their own techniques to further boost its effects especially when it comes to cognitive behavioral therapy. This combination has been proven to be quite effective when it comes to helping people gain better perspective and control over their maladaptive, irrational and self-defeating thoughts.

How to Get Started on your Own

If you cannot attend a group session or have no spare cash to get a guide to teach you how to practice it, don't fret. There are simple yet effective methods through which you can do mindfulness meditation.

These involve concentration, breathing practices and observing our thoughts. As simple as these may seem, they are known to be effective especially when it comes to placing us in a calmer state of mind.

Aside from these, you may also want to try more physical methods such as yoga or Tai chi. These methods can induce a relaxation response whilst exercising our body as well, releasing any tension in our muscles and relieving the pain caused by it.

Concentration Exercises:

Following the flow. When it comes to mindfulness meditation, it is important that you first establish concentration and allow yourself to observe the flow of your emotions, inner thoughts and different bodily sensations without overthinking it or judging whether they are good or bad.

Be attentive. As you focus, you will begin to notice different external sensations as touch, sound and sight. These are the things that make up each moment and give life to every encounter you have. The challenge now is to not get attached to any of these things or to one particular idea and emotion that it brings up. Whenever we latch on to these things, we become caught up in thinking about the past or the future and find ourselves becoming affected by it - often negatively. Instead, pay attention but don't engage anything that you think or feel. In becoming an observer, you form a detachment, which allows you to separate yourself from the negativity that these things may bring.

Practice. For beginners, especially, the process may not always feel relaxing or calming. Thoughts can be disruptive at times especially if you're experiencing a lot of stress in that particular moment. Don't worry if you don't get the hang of it immediately. This always takes time and a bit of warm up before you ease into that state of mind. With constant practice, however, you should be able to do it easily and with a greater range of self-awareness when it comes to your experiences.

Do these three exercises everyday whenever you have a bit of time to spare. Half an hour is more than enough to pull you away from negative and stressful thinking, allowing your mind to focus more on the present. What you get is clarity, peace of mind and more motivation to do what is needed at the moment.

Chapter 14: Mindfulness.

Mindfulness is an awareness that arises through intentionally attending in an open, accepting and discerning way to whatever is arising in the present moment. The mind illuminates everything that arises at every point in time in every moment of a human life. Mindfulness deals with keeping human consciousness alive to the present reality, but as humans are fully aware of what happens around them, they remain unaffected by them in their present life. It therefore involves the disregard of the present reality of the environment or world where a human exists with all the conditions or situations that he may find himself. So, while the human person observes the present realities of continuous and ongoing internal and external stimuli as they arise in his world and environment, he does not react to them at all but ignores them completely and intentionally.

Mindfulness is a path or way by which a human being can promote mindful presence, attending to immediate experience with care and discernment, living with our whole being. Mindfulness is a self-awareness training adapted from Buddhist mindfulness meditation. It has been adapted for use in the treatment of depression, especially preventing relapse and for assisting with mood regulation. It has been described as a state of being in the present, accepting things for what they are (i.e. being non-judgmental). It was originally developed to assist with mood regulation and relapse prevention in depression and has been found to have considerable health benefits.

Mindfulness is therefore a practice where a human person purposely focuses his attention strictly on the present moment at every point in time and accepting the reality of the condition or situation without judgment nor reaction. It has been examined scientifically and has been proven to be a key factor in the attainment of happiness, mood or personality of a human person.

In a human life, Physical and Emotional pain is inevitable. It is believed that humans suffer when confronted with beliefs and attitudes. Humans become caught up in such beliefs and attitudes and it becomes rather impossible to let go. Such beliefs and attitudes become unacceptable and eventually humans get consumed by these beliefs and attitudes that it becomes very difficult to take a rational action. A human person tries very hard to be in full control of his life, but often time gets overwhelmed by these learned patterns of unacceptable situations and conditions which results into pain and suffering.

However, every human possesses the ability to be mindful, i.e. having total control over those beliefs and attitudes that cause pain and suffering when we deal with the situations and conditions that we find ourselves. Humans can develop a clear mind by imbibing and mastering the ability to separate and disengage from those stimuli that cause confusion by training the mind to fully pay attention to each present moment. So instead of reacting instantly to those confusing stimuli, the human person will be able to respond appropriately to the condition and situation since his decision making process has been improved and he can easily attain mental and physical relaxation.

Through mindfulness, a human person can learn to pay attention on purpose by practicing specially developed mindfulness meditation practices and movements (this includes among others, qigong, chanting, meditations, yoga, tai chi etc.). These practices and movements will help a human person to master control over his body both intrinsically and extrinsically. The person will learn how to slow down or stop brain chatter and automatic or habitual reactions, experiencing the present moment as it really is. In the process of such practices and movements, unsolicited thoughts will flow to the person freely as a normal function of the brain. This thoughts are bound to come in and there is nothing the human person can do to avoid them, but mindfulness practices cauterize the importance of how the human person responds to such thoughts. Once the person starts to ponder, reflect and deliberate on the thoughts as they flow into his head, he may become angry and frustrated at himself for not being able to retain his focus. This means that his attention on the present moment has been interfered with. But where the person merely allows and acknowledges the thoughts and does away with it as quickly as possible as the thoughts comes in without judgment, they will be able to maintain focus on the present moment.

We can therefore reckon that mindfulness is the practice where a human person deliberately directs his attention to what occurs in his mind at every point in time. It is a practice where the human person realizes his conditioning, how he is moved by urges and desires to obtain pleasure and avoid pain, how his thought processes are influenced, impacted and eventually changes. This is because what a human person thinks of his "Self" constantly changes. Human efforts to maintain an identity leads to suffering, this is because of the reactions and interference with the immediate realities which man is prone to make so as to fit the realities into his conceptions. However, by the means of mindfulness, a human person can attain a level of freedom and peace through acceptance of his immediate realities.

Every person, through constant practicing of the movements and other practices of mindfulness can master the skill. Once the skill is mastered, a person can learn how to remain calm and always be in control of his mind, even in the midst of any problem or difficult situation that he finds himself. Instead of being fearful, thinking negatively, being anxious or expecting the worst (all these amount to pain and sufferings as explained above), which may define the mood of the person by making him sad, agitated or unsatisfied, the person can through the practice of mindfulness choose to be mentally and emotionally stable, poised and unshaken. At this point, the person will attain a good level of peace of mind (as explained above), his inner strength will be reinforced and his self-confidence will be boosted.

Chapter 15: What Is Mindfulness?

Mindfulness: Ancient Meaning

According to ancient texts, "mindfulness" is derived from the word, **sati**, a Pali term, which refers to attention, remembering, and awareness. Pali has been the language for interpreting and teaching the lessons of the Buddha. It is said that in 1921, **sati** was translated into "mindfulness" to better understand its concept. At the same time, the meaning of "mindfulness" has also been modified for psychotherapy application. Today, it now includes a wide range of concepts as well as practices.

Aspects of Mindfulness

While awareness is inexplicitly powerful, attention is more powerful given that it denotes focused awareness. When you are aware of what transpires within and around you, you will be able to start to disengage yourself from difficult emotion and mental preoccupation. In some instances, disengaging from suffering or a demanding situation is quite simple. Take the case of a mentally retarded individual. Just because he is developmentally challenged does not mean he cannot manage his anger. A mentally retarded individual may simply shift his attention to the palms of his hands once he notices he is angry. Consequently, instead of suppressing or controlling intense emotions, human beings can redirect their attention in order to manage how they feel.

"Remembering" is another aspect of mindfulness. The term "remembering" does not refer to recalling the past. "Remembering" entails being aware and paying attention, focusing on the significance of intention in practicing mindfulness. Simply put, this aspect entails reminding oneself "to remember to become aware" in every moment or situation.

On the other hand, "mindfulness" is more than just being aware for the sake of being so. According to Buddhist scholars, **attention**, **remembering** (**sati**), and **awareness** are all present, say, when a thief takes aim at his victim with malevolence in his heart. This is not the goal of Buddhist psychology or what psychotherapists try to foster. The purpose of mindfulness based on its ancient or original discourse is to discard unnecessary suffering through nourishing insight into the material world's nature and the workings of the mind. Practicing mindfulness involves working with the states of mind for the purpose of abiding peacefully in whatever circumstance one is in.

Individuals are able to manage their minds, developing the ability to become "street smart" through mindfulness. It aids in recognizing when to cultivate mental qualities, including concentration, effort, alertness, kindness, and loving in order to alleviate suffering in a skillful manner. For instance, if you feel lazy, you may try to increase your energy level either in your mind or body or if you are self-critical during meditation, you may incorporate a little compassion.

It should be noted that mindfulness is not a stand-alone formula to alleviate or discard suffering. Mindfulness alone is insufficient for achieving happiness. However, it establishes a solid groundwork for various factors. Rather than addressing mindfulness as a goal in itself, the classical literature usually discussed it based on its function. It is a significant part of a project, which is intended to displace habits of the mind that are entrenched and cause unhappiness, including unpleasant emotions of greed, anger, or envy, or behaviors that cause harm to oneself and others.

Meanwhile, in psychotherapy, the recent focus on mindfulness is a strategic rectification to some modern trends in treatment. More often than not, therapists, even those with the purest intentions, are inclined to "correct" the problems of the patients while unknowingly bypassing self-understanding and self-acceptance.

In the next chapters, it will be demonstrated that human behavioral and emotional problems are factors that can be magnified through one's instinctive efforts to alleviate discomfort by impelling into activities that seek change. The modern approach of a mindfulness-oriented agenda is first and foremost, awareness and acceptance, followed by change.

Problems Encountered During Mindfulness Meditation

While practicing mindfulness meditation, it is normal to encounter problems or difficulties; however, it is best not let them upset you. When you encounter problems during meditation, view them as an opportunity to figure out where your unskillful habits are instead of viewing them as a sign of not making progress. In addition, avoid perceiving these problems as a sign that it is hopeless for you to become a meditator. These problems are great opportunities to learn how to respond appropriately to the unskillful members of your mind's committee. Consequently, when you view these problems positively, you develop your discernment. In fact, in dealing with the most common problems in meditation, specifically pain and wandering thoughts, many people were brought to their awakening.

External Noises

When meditating and you find yourself fretting about external noises, tell yourself that the noise does not affect you. This is also saying that you are the one who is bothering the noise. You should keep in mind that external noises do not have the intention to bother you while you are meditating. More so, think of your body as a cover on a huge window while the noise is like the wind that goes through you. Simply put, you do not need to offer resistance to the external noises. What you should do is to let the noises get through you instead of towards you.

Avoid letting yourself get affected by the external noises. Visualize them as passing right through you with making any contact, both physically and mentally.

Wandering Thoughts

One of the most basic habits of the mind is to create worlds of thoughts and then live in those worlds. It would be extremely useful to apply the concept of **becoming**, which the Buddha taught his disciples. **Becoming** allows you to utilize your imagination to contemplate the lessons from the past as well as plan for the future. However, the skill of **becoming** can also be destructive given that you tend to create worlds of thoughts, which lead to the development of aversion, greed, delusion, and other mental habits that are destructive. For instance, when you are able to relive the past, you are inclined to being miserable in your present state. In the same way, when you are able to plan for the future, you are inclined to developing worries, which can overcome your peace of mind.

In order to deal with wandering thoughts, you can implement five simple strategies. Each of these strategies allows you to strengthen your concentration as well as teach lessons in discernment. These strategies include: return to the breath; ignore the thoughts; suppress the thoughts; focus on the drawbacks of staying with the distractions; and relax the tension, which keeps the thought going.

Pain

Pain is inevitable as you practice meditation. Throughout your meditation course, pain will either turn on or off. As such, you need to perceive it with discernment and equanimity. Take it as something that normally transpires. It would not help if you dwell too much on the pain. Instead, drop the term "pain" and replace it with "pains" given that there are various types of pain. When you learn the difference among these types of pain, you develop discernment with regard to the workings of the mind.

Other common problems that you may encounter during your practice of meditation include drowsiness, delusion concentration, and external noises.

Drowsiness

Once you feel sleepy during your practice of meditation, do not take it as a sign that you have to rest. More often than not, drowsiness is the mind's way to avoid an issue, which is about to come out from your inner profundity. You may want to know first about the deeper issues in your inner depths prior to regarding drowsiness as a sign to rest. As a someone who meditates, you need to test this drowsiness once you encounter it.

You can test it by changing the topic of your meditation. You can do this by changing the breath's texture and rhythm. You can also change the area of focus. You can also change your posture. Instead of assuming the sitting posture, you can get up and do the standing and/or walking meditation. If you are still drowsy, the body might be implying that it needs some rest.

Delusion Concentration

This common problem encountered during meditation is also associated with drowsiness. It is a state of mind in which it is still; however, the mind is not aware of where your attention is centered. When you come out of delusion concentration, you are inclined to wonder if you were awake or asleep while meditating.

Delusion concentration happens when the breath becomes too comfortable without spreading your awareness to your other body parts. You tend to focus your attention on a small area. Thus, when the breath in that specific area gets too comfortable or refined, you tend to lose track of the breath and slip into a pleasant yet blurry state of mind.

In order to prevent experiencing delusion concentration, you can immediately begin surveying the rest of your body as soon as your breathing becomes comfortable.

Take note of how the breath energy flows in all the points, spots, areas, or parts of the body regardless if it is down to the spots between your toes and fingers. You can also envision the different body parts such as the organs and the bones. Take note if the breath energy spreads smoothly into those parts.

Chapter 16: The Secrets To Eliminate Distractions

Practicing mindfulness also means that you have to start letting go of distractions.

Distractions are just temptations, and you know what happened when Eve bit that fruit.

They only keep you away from what you're supposed to be, and how you're supposed to feel. Basically, if you learn how to let go of things that distract you, even for just a while,

you'll be able to concentrate on what you're supposed to do. Follow some of the suggestions:

1. Take some time out from social media. Sometimes, what you see online may just

irritate you, which will lead to not being able to finish your task right away. Being away from social media, even for just a day or so, would already make you feel a

lot better about yourself, and would make you realize how great life actually is.

2. Don't eat while working, especially if you're not hungry. Sometimes, food can

become your comfort object - and that's not a good thing. You have to eat when it's time, and not all the time.

3. Stop thinking of that movie you're going to watch if you still have work to finish.

Focus on the now.

Learn the Basics of Mindfulness

Of course, it's best to begin with the basics. In order to perfume basic mindfulness, which is all about calming the mind, and allowing yourself to enter that state of self-awareness

and acceptance¼

Here's what you could do.

1. Sit down comfortably on a mat or on the floor, and focus on your own sense of

breathing. Just breathe - you actually don't have to do deep-breathing - or try to count your breaths. Just breathe and focus on how it's happening. Feel it coming through your nose, by your throat, even in the chest and diaphragm.

2. Feel your breaths. By doing so, you're kept grounded and you get to the point

where you see that breathing is actually amazing and that it's something that keeps you alive.

3. Bring your attention back to your breathing. Sometimes your mind may wander

off and it's best to just cut it out and focus on breathing again. Don't criticize yourself, though. Just tell yourself that you're breathing. Focus on that.

You could also try Shamatha Mindfulness, which goes like this:

1. Sit down and tell yourself that at this moment, you are going to work for the

betterment of your mind. Sit upright and make sure that your feet touch the

ground. Or sit down on the floor or on a yoga mat with your legs crossed to feel stable and strong.

2. Be in an erect position - your shoulders should be on the same level with each

other.

3. Look down ¼ just a couple of inches from your nose. Make sure that you don't get

distracted by looking at other things.

4. Just relax and breathe. Don't think about anything else and focus only on your

breathing patterns. Imagine how each breath flows throughout each part of your body.

If any thought comes up, tell yourself to stop thinking about it because it does not belong

in this moment. Focus on that. Afterward, you could utter the following affirmations:

1. I am brilliant, and I can do a lot.

2. I am the stylist of my life. I can always change my life to a better direction.

3. I am happy - and hard times will pass.

4. I am a brave person, and I will not allow any interference from destroyers.

5. I will let go of things that pull me down.

6. I am full of grace.

7. I'll be able to reach my goals in time.

8. In a couple of years, I'll be able to move into a new house, and travel.

9. I am on the path to success and greatness.

10. I'll be able to achieve my dreams.

Remember to try practicing this daily, and once you get the hang of it, you can move on to other mindfulness exercises. You can also try other meditative exercises even as early as the present because you might get to focus on them more. Check out the next chapters to see what this means.

Chapter 17: Living A Healthier Lifestyle- Making Mindful Choices

Our bodies are exposed to external stress daily through air pollution, sun damage, contaminated water, and more. Modern life is stressful before we even get to work in the morning most of the time. Often we may find ourselves eating whatever our body is craving, with common culprits being sugar, empty carbs, processed foods, and eating too much. But in the end, this is not going to make us feel any better or improve our lives in any way.

Learning to eat in a sustainable way is important for good health and feeling good overall. Nutrition is one of the key components to how well our body will function. Foods that do not contribute to good nutrition often contribute to issues such as obesity, diabetes, cancer and other diseases. Lack of essential nutrients is a serious detriment to your health, physically and mentally.

Nutrient deficiency is also known to cause depression, mood swings, irritability, and lack of focus. If the body is fed junk food all of the time, the endocrine system, which regulates our hormones, is on a constant swing up and down. The junk food disrupts this system, which will affect our overall health. Foods of little nutritional value are lower vibrational foods that do not contribute to elevating your consciousness. High vibrational foods, such as fruits, vegetables, and superfoods like spirulina not only nourish the body but help facilitate the natural cleansing and detoxification process that happens to keep our bodies healthy.

When the body is unhealthy, the mind will be too. Why not take care of your body now? It's the only one you have. If you notice that what you eat is draining you and not providing the essential energy you need, you have to take a stance and learn to say no to what does not serve you.

We must ensure that our body receives enough protein, vitamins, minerals and healthy fats to provide essential energy. If you are feeling unsatisfied about your physical condition and/or even your mental state (i.e. suffering from depression/anxiety), one of the first things you can do is look at your diet. What is lacking? What is there too much of? Is there something in particular contributing to your health dilemma?

Sugar

Sugar addiction is on the rise in Western society and is one of the biggest hidden health issues out there today. It is not only used as a hidden booster in many foods but also the main ingredient in cheap foods found at quick-stop convenience stores today. The truth is that mindful eating is not a quick and easy path. Instead of grabbing that candy bar on your way from work to the gym when you're in a hungry pinch, plan better by packing carrot sticks or apples. Instead of eating donuts for breakfast, opt for fresh fruit with yogurt. And ditch the soda habit!

Sugar addiction is a leading cause of obesity, diabetes, and mood/energy swings. Sugar without proper proteins and carbs transforms into glucose, which causes a spike in blood sugar. This what happens when you feel a sugar rush. But soon, that feeling is over and you crash.

When you are addicted to sugar, you will crave it and overeat it. The sugar response tells your brain that it makes you feel good, therefore tricking yourself into thinking you want more. It can be a challenge to break a sugar habit, but with a little mindfulness, you will find the path to success. The best way to kick the sugar habit is to address what in your diet contains sugar. Eliminate 1 item per week until you are completely sugar-free. You must adjust your taste buds to get used to not eating sweets all the time! Set yourself up for success from the very beginning.

Once you have eliminated a sugar problem, you can begin to feel your own natural energy, which is a very rewarding and satisfying feeling. Also by making healthy food choices, you will feel better about yourself, your brain will feel happier and your body will thank you.

It was not long ago that I was living outside of San Francisco and indulging in too much food all the time. While many people's vices are sweet sugar-filled products, mine was actually carbs and cheese. Pizza, pasta, chips, white cheddar- you can bet they were a part of my weekly diet. I was certainly not getting enough nutrients from fruits and vegetables.

This is, in fact, another form of sugar addiction. When your body craves carbs, it can sometimes secretly be a sugar addiction. Carbohydrates turn into glucose, which causes your blood sugar to rise. This isn't to say that all carbs are bad, however. Simple carbohydrates break down much quicker than complex carbohydrates, so it is important to choose the ones which will be better for you.

One of the greatest gifts in this life is our ability to make choices. Sometimes we may not have control over certain situations, but we do have the choice to control how we respond. It is important to always take a moment to look at whatever is affecting us so we can make the choices that will impact us on the most positive note.

"Life is a matter of choices, and every choice you make makes you." —John C. Maxwell

When we consider the choices at hand to any dilemma, we can weigh the pros and cons. How will our reaction serve us or not serve our needs? If we do not give our self the space to decide, then we have robbed ourselves of that choice and allowed a lower sense of self to operate. Have you regretted a decision you made rashly without giving it too much thought?

Our choices have power. Once we understand that, we can learn to use them to our advantage, whether it's through our food choices or how we respond to pressure at work, etc. A habit is an unconscious choice. This can be both a good and bad thing. When we unconsciously make good choices, we are nourishing ourselves. But if we have a bad habit that is not promoting our health, then we must first become aware of the choice we are making to be unhealthy over and over again. Then we must make a choice to break that unwanted habit.

"Life is about choices. Some we regret, some we're proud of. Some will haunt us forever. The message: we are what we chose to be." —Graham Brown

Quitting Bad Habits

While I was in Peru, I quit caffeine. I had been addicted to caffeine my entire adult life. It was something I felt guilty about and something I struggled with. I felt like I didn't know myself without my morning coffee. If I didn't have coffee within my first hour or so of waking, I would inevitably have a headache and be unable to go through my day. That wasn't who I was! I had too much to do to feel like that. So it became a vicious cycle I could never break. The only days I never had caffeine were sick days. And as soon as I was better enough to get out of bed, it was back to the coffee.

The ayahuasca diet required eliminating caffeine. I knew this was going to be a struggle for me. Even in the past when I had done other detox diets like a juice cleanse, I still drank green tea in the morning. However, for whatever reason, I successfully weaned myself off coffee almost effortlessly- and I think my traveling journey had something to do with it.

One stressful thing about traveling was always having to wake up and find the nearest coffee source. Although a cup o' Joe is not expensive usually, they do add up over time. And they had added up quite a bit over my lifetime. Back in the United States, my caffeine habit had turned into a morning espresso habit, and not in a good way, but in the Starbucks double shot kind of way. These were basically little cans of sugary caffeinated goodness. When I had to regularly wake up early, I would down one of these bad boys in an instant and be ready to go.

Regular coffee and tea always made me go to the bathroom way too much. These things? Not so much since it was such a quick fix. The downsides? They really hurt my stomach and were NOT healthy at all! I think my excessive consumption of them during my last year in the US added to my weight gain. I actually began to simply mix espresso powder with almond milk toward the end of this phase instead of the Double Shots, which helped with my stomach issues. However, I was still almost always hit with afternoon fatigue—which meant more caffeine.

It was a constant up and down cycle that I struggled through. Often, because I would then drink caffeine so late during the day, I would then be unable to sleep at night. Which became another long-standing battle with sleeping pills. I felt even further away from knowing myself at the end of the day.

At this point, I was finishing up a yoga-teaching contract in Nicaragua at a resort. My daily routine was to be one of the first people in the restaurant for my cup of coffee. I would usually sit by the ocean to sip it or sometimes I would take it to the yoga platform to enjoy before teaching my first class of the day.

Since my life was fairly relaxing at this time and I only had 2 classes per day I was teaching (one in the morning and a gentle class in the evening), I told myself that it was okay to be a little more tired in the afternoon. Who wants a hyperactive yoga teacher anyways, right? I got myself down to just 1 cup of coffee per day within a matter of weeks. And what a difference it made!

By the time I got to Peru, however, I was extremely exhausted. It was only a matter of days before my ceremony and I still hadn't completely kicked the habit. I was doing a homestay in Lima during my first few days and I ended up needing to take a few extra days there to just let myself be tired. During the days of the ceremonies, I never found myself wanting coffee or caffeinated tea. And afterward, that feeling stayed with me. After a week had gone by, I realized that I had really quit caffeine! I could do it.

It has taken me some time to get used to life without caffeine. I have to be careful about tea and have learned how to politely turn it down. It's so interesting that something I used to love so much I actually have no desire to partake in anymore.

Again, this has to do with drastically lowering my stress levels. I no longer have to drive around a city and sit in traffic to go to work. I always teach yoga within walking distance of where I live during my contracts in foreign countries and I work online- which I can do anywhere, anytime. I have had to learn how to honor when I am tired. Being tired was something I often did not like and did not want to feel. However, when I was going through the severe caffeine/sleeping pill phase, I often napped not only once, but twice a day. My whole system was completely messed up. Almost all of my free time was spent wasted, napping, instead of working to pursue other projects I truly love.

I have always been a self-starter and enjoy working for myself the best, so this was not a healthy lifestyle for me. Even though I was technically "doing things I loved" and making money at them, I was clearly still struggling internally and with my health, which meant things were out of balance. Since I have quit caffeine, I actually now have WAY more energy to pursue the things I love to do and have put the steps in place to make my business ideas a reality.

Not to mention some of the other added bonuses- less stomach pain, less dry mouth, less having to run to the bathroom, less feeling like my heart is going to explode all the time, and less up and down with my energy levels. I actually sleep MUCH better. And when I do feel tired in the afternoon, I now challenge myself to hula hoop or move my body. And guess what? It works!

Being Authentic

When I decided to take my first job teaching abroad in Nicaragua, many of my family and even close friends objected. They thought I was acting irrationally and making a decision without thinking it all the way through. I had just shipped all of my belongings across the country from California to Florida, back to where my family lived.

I went to visit my family before I left. The second my flight landed in Florida, I was met with resistance. Everyone thought I was making a mistake, acting on impulse and trying to run away from my problems.

To be fair, I was undergoing a huge emotional toll that was causing me to lash out at times. People thought I was unstable. My family actually recommended mental health care help to me and that I needed to stop pursuing the things I loved as a career. They thought I had reached the end of the line. But I knew deep inside that I hadn't. And I knew I had to remain true to myself, even despite the odds against me.

It was in this moment that it was difficult for me to find my flow. Should I stay in Florida and move home for the second time of my adult life and try to find a normal job making decent money I would probably miserable at? Or should I go to Nicaragua, into the unknown, to a place where people feared for my safety and my future was uncertain?

These were the questions I asked myself over and over again. I even delayed my flight by 2 weeks to make sure I was really making the right choice. I was trying to flow with my intuition like water through a stream, but giant river rocks kept appearing in my way. So the time came where I had to make the critical decision about what I was going to do- and I chose to take a risk in order to live authentically. I didn't want to play it safe anymore. I know that I'm better at making it up as I go along anyways.

Creative problem solving has always been my specialty! And when you learn to apply it to your life... things just get better. Maybe you shouldn't take risks and go to faraway countries like I did, but then again, maybe you should! A lot of being authentic is asking yourself the right questions, and most of us aren't asking the right questions or thinking big picture.

Find Awareness Through Your Choices

Bring yourself into the present moment

What will be the benefits and pitfalls of your choice?

How do you feel about this decision? Notice how your emotions play a role in making your choice

Does your choice honor and reflect your personal values?

Ask yourself how this choice will affect your life in the short and long-term

Chapter 18: 7 Days Of Mindfulness

1. MINDFUL BREATHING

TIME REQUIRED

8 minutes daily for at least a week (though evidence suggests that mindfulness increases the more you practice it).

Stress, anger, and anxiety can impair not only our health but our judgment and skills of attention. Fortunately, research suggests an effective way to deal with these difficult feelings: the practice of "mindfulness," the ability to pay careful attention to what you're thinking, feeling, and sensing in the present moment without judging those thoughts and feelings as good or bad. Countless studies link mindfulness to better health, lower anxiety, and greater resilience to stress.

But how do you cultivate mindfulness? A basic method is to focus your attention on your own breathing—a practice called, quite simply, "mindful breathing." After setting aside time to practice mindful breathing, you should find it easier to focus attention on your breath in your daily life—an important skill to help you deal with stress, anxiety, and negative emotions, cool yourself down when your temper flares, and sharpen your skills of concentration.

Mindfulness gives people distance from their thoughts and feelings, which can help them tolerate and work through unpleasant feelings rather than becoming overwhelmed by them. Mindful breathing in particular is helpful because it gives people an anchor--their breath--on which they can focus when they find themselves carried away by a stressful thought. Mindful breathing also helps people stay "present" in the moment, rather than being distracted by regrets in the past or worries about the future.

The most basic way to do mindful breathing is simply to focus your attention on your breath, the inhale and exhale. You can do this while standing, but ideally you'll be sitting or even lying in a comfortable position. Your eyes may be open or closed, but you may find it easier to maintain your focus if you close your eyes. It can help to set aside a designated time for this exercise, but it can also help to practice it when you're feeling particularly stressed or anxious. Experts believe a regular practice of mindful breathing can make it easier to do it in difficult situations.

Sometimes, especially when trying to calm yourself in a stressful moment, it might help to start by taking an exaggerated breath: a deep inhale through your nostrils (3 seconds), hold your breath (2 seconds), and a long exhale through your mouth (4 seconds). Otherwise, simply observe each breath without trying to adjust it; it may help to focus on the rise and fall of your chest or the sensation through your nostrils. As you do so, you may find that your mind wanders, distracted by thoughts or bodily sensations. That's OK. Just notice that this is happening and gently bring your attention back to your breath.

Chapter 19: Mindfulness Meditation Techniques

The power is within you to create your own happiness. You, alone can master your mind, and with mindfulness meditation, it is possible. Look around you, everything that you see around you, they were created by the creative energy of your own thoughts. You have created, you are creating, and will be creating your own reality. Every person's thoughts are powerful channels that help transform any idea into physical reality.

You Have the Power to Create

When you feel confident about the things that you can do, and about yourself as a whole, embracing your talents and the resources you have comes easy, which is the first step towards realizing your full potential. You attain personal power by first wishing to achieve something, and acting on them, starting from where you are right now up to where you want to go. Your enthusiasm helps propel you to what you want to do.

Do you know who you are?

To release your inner power, you need to know who you truly are. Dig deep and get re-acquainted with you who are. Self-knowledge is the key to "unleashing" your power to create.

Think about where you are in your life right now. If you had a choice, where would you want to be in 10 years? In 20 years?

Now, think about where you are and what you have in your life right now if you didn't have to deal with the "buts" and the "what ifs".

What drives you? What makes you happy? What will make you happy? What do you do when you there is nothing much going on? If you have difficulty providing answers for these questions, you are most likely to simply drift through life: with no purpose, no goal, no passion, only driven by the wind, and just letting the blowing of the wind take you anywhere.

Each one of us has a purpose in life. Some people may recognize it, while there are some who can't seem to find that purpose.

Do you know what you really want? What would you do to achieve those goals and desires?

When you have a vivid idea of what you want to with your life and where you want to go, you begin to access your personal power. The key is to focusing on what you want. You shouldn't have to worry about what other people say and want for you. When you are sure about what your goals are, no amount of persuasion or discouragement that you get from other people can stop you from realizing those goals. This is true confidence. This is tapping into your inner power. You have the power to create your own reality!

Having a clear vision of what you want, you can easily set how you would realize them. The universe will not wait until you are ready to set a goal and work on achieving that goal, it is you who have to call the shots. Until you take control, the universe cannot act on them.

Having a vivid image of where you want to go and what you want to do lets you focus your energy on those goals, and the universe has no other choice but to respond.

Lose the Negativity

Most people are more prone to dwelling on the negatives – worries, challenges, and disadvantages – that are believed to keep them from achieving their desires. They fail to realize that the more they think about them, the more they make their dreams impossible to reach, simply because all their energies are geared towards thinking about these negatives.

These are the times that you do not have the power and you end up failing and becoming the victim, instead of becoming the victor who overcomes the challenges.

The first step is to recognize the habitual excuses that you have in your head that let you run away from the challenges. It is one thing to know what you actually want, it's another to figure out what hinders you from getting it. Write down the reasons that prevent you from pursuing the things that you want: lack of time, you can't do it, it's expensive, or you don't know what to do. Negative thoughts like these do not, in any way, help you to achieve your hopes and dreams.

Of course you'll have to find time for the things that you want to achieve. Working for what you want to achieve doesn't come with a price but when you do reach your goal and you become the person you want to be, it will be worth all the trouble.

Do you want your purpose in life is?

To achieve your goals, you have to have a definite purpose and stick with it. What do you want to achieve 10 years from now? With persistence and determination, and passion and drive in doing whatever it takes to achieve that purpose, there is no way that you won't succeed.

Everything starts in your mind. Realize that thought is energy and that energy is power. Believe that you can achieve whatever you put your mind into. Mental strength can be achieved through constant practice. Start with the small things. Visualize what you want and then let go. Let the universe work its way around those goals.

When you can do it with the smaller goals, you can add your most ardent desires, the ones that you want to achieve for your life in the years to come.

Visualization may be seeing your future and it is power. When you visualize yourself already realizing your dreams, you begin to feel it, and you begin to be in it – you are living your dreams. Wouldn't it be exciting to see them slowly unfold in your day to day life? Some people fail to focus on what's in front of them, so they often miss out on the daily triumphs that they have, en route to their ultimate life goal.

Unless you become mindful of the now, you won't feel that you are growing every single day.

Remember that the power is within you. What you have to do is tap into that inner power through mindfulness meditation exercises and you can create the best future ever.

Mastering Your Mind

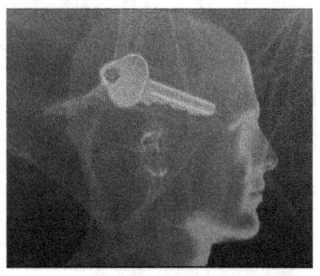

The key to mastering the mind is to practice mindfulness meditation. Many people fail to realize that meditation can alter the way we think as "stable" mental traits. Aside from relaxation and calmness, meditation and mindfulness combined can be used as a tool to investigate your mind and thoughts, in order to change how you view the world.

You need to begin looking into how the mind works, so that you can change your thoughts, one step at a time.

Attention: How to Stabilize the Mind

When you are used to living in this generation of computers, video games, smart phone apps, telemarketing calls, and endless emails, it is easy to overlook some of the most important things in life, like actually living! Your mind is always preoccupied that you don't have time to just sit, do nothing, and free the mind. Today, even kids are not used to not tinkering with their game consoles and tablets.

The modern life definitely succeeds in distracting everyone. However, the problem may not be your cellular phone or your laptop, but in yourself. After all, you are one who constantly chooses what to prioritize and what to set aside. The trouble probably lies in not choosing the ones that need to be legitimately prioritized.

By nature, the mind is rather unstable, but meditation can stabilize it. How is that possible? Meditation is all about paying attention, and mindfulness meditation is paying attention to the present moment. Aside from stabilizing your mind, it promotes clarity, improves creativity, and helps boost productivity. Even your relationships will greatly improve when you practice mindfulness meditation – just think about how happy you would be if you could give your undivided, 100% attention to your spouse?

The trick is to start you with mindfulness techniques, which aim to cultivate nonjudgmental awareness of a chosen object and seeing deeply into everything. In the sample exercise presented to you in the previous chapters, the object of focus is your breathing, noting every time you take in and every time you expel air, and patiently returning your attention to your breathing in instances when your mind would wander.

Learning how to focus on a single object allows you to observe the influx of moment-to-moment perception. When you consistently practice, you will be seeing the patterns behind fluctuations.

The goal is to flex the muscles in your brain and mindfulness meditation helps strengthen and stabilize your brain's main control center called the medial prefrontal cortex, which is responsible for regulating your attention. Exercising the brain muscles will result in the balance awareness between distraction and dullness. This is achieved by a self-monitoring process called metacognition, or awareness of awareness. It alerts you when on one side, your attention begins to drift off and brings you back with renewed interest; and on the other end, when you are distracted and you need to shift back your attention.

This is a process the enhance concentration, and as you continue to fine-tune it, there will be habitual chaos in your mind, but they will gradually taper down to bring calmness and clarity.

How to Recognize the Spark that Signals the Flame

You may not recognize it but much of your emotional experience is brought about by negative feelings that were "blown" into your brain. When these negative feelings manifest, that's when you experience emotions; but the truth is, emotions cannot be considered as facts.

When you let these negative feelings rule your mind, they become your worst enemies, clouding your mind, and preventing you from seeing, feeling, and responding with utmost clarity. They simply distract you from living your life to the fullest.

However, a lot of people fail to recognize the mental anguish and opt to continue to suffer from the pain of yesterday, the pain of today, and the pain of the future.

When you practice mindfulness meditation, it zeroes in on your relationship with your emotions rather than the emotions themselves. You get to see various mood fluctuations by the moment, making it easier for you to navigate through them. So, instead of being the storm, you become the sky, and you avoid the mental judgment or acting on impulse.

It is never easy to recognize the emotional triggers, because for most people, the lag time between provocation and action is actually shorter than a heartbeat. In just a fraction of a section, your emotions can immediately swamp your judgment, and most of the time, your emotions succeed.

With mindfulness meditation, you develop the ability to recognize the "spark just before the flame". When you learn to observe how your emotions work, leading to the quieting of the mind, you also become more familiar when emotions arise, and how they can disappear without too much impact or greatly overwhelming your mind.

"Seeing" Your Mind Allows You to "See" Other People's Minds

Meditation helps cultivate intimacy with your own state of mind. Mindfulness is a special kind of intrapersonal attunement, making it the perfect tool to develop compassion for others. When you learn to see through your own mind, you also learn how to see through other people's minds.

Compassion is one of the hardest to practice because it is hard to be compassionate to somebody who may have been hostile towards you, while asking for your help.

During meditation, you simply practice over and over again. You simply learn to love a particular person, wish for their well-being, and gladly extend a helping hand to other people; and this may also include the people you might consider your enemies.

So, your next step is to the next thing to do is to extend that feeling of compassion to other people. Let compassion grow and inhabit your mind so that your whole being develops compassion, benevolence, and loving kindness for humanity. You just keep on doing it until it becomes a part of your life, not just while meditating, but it becomes second nature that you don't need the aid of meditation to "go into a state of compassion". Once it becomes a part of what you are, it's going to be easy.

Every human being has the inner ability of empathy and compassion, but because of our judgmental nature, we tend to block those positive feelings off (albeit unconsciously) because of past hurts. But mindfulness meditation can help you with refocusing your mind until it becomes second nature to you.

Happiness: You Deserve It

One of the benefits of practicing mindfulness meditation is calmness, relaxation, joy, and happiness. How is happiness possible? It's because when your mind is clear, you have less negative thoughts so you minimize negative behaviors, you become less anxious, so you experience more of what life has to offer, and that can bring happiness.

When you have a happy disposition, you become more productive at work because you are not fazed by challenges. When this happens, you get to achieve your personal goals and you reach your full potential.

Buddhism (where meditation and mindfulness somewhat originated) teaches us that lasting happiness is our birthright. However, happiness doesn't come from having, but rather from freeing ourselves of afflictive emotions and mental "blindness". The joy of achieving inner freedom and learning to develop genuine love and kindness for humanity radiates from within towards others, that is true happiness!

Remember that awareness can bring you your life back. It's up to you how to live that life!

Chapter 20: Getting To Know Mindfulness

Mindfulness is basically the ability to live in the moment. It means living every moment purposefully and with intention through lenses of compassion, acceptanceand curiosity. It sounds both simple and complex, and that's because it's both. Through mindfulness, you can make the most out of every moment in your life.

Mindfulness is not just a practice that you can do at certain stretches; it can also be a lifestyle that you can live by. You can find ways to make your life much more than it is by living mindfully. This chapter is about what mindfulness is, and its origins. This will also prepare you for your mindfulness journey.

What is Mindfulness?

Although it was developed in the east, it has been gaining ground in the west and is becoming more and more popular everyday. It was in the early 1980's when mindfulness was developed as a way of therapy. This concept explores the probability of a happier and healthier life through positivity and calmness.

Mindfulness can be considered as a translation of *Sati*, an Indian word which means *awareness, attention and remembrance*, all of which are key parts of mindfulness. Mindfulness originated from Buddhist teaching and brings these key aspects into consciousness.

Awareness pertains to how you perceive your present experiences and how conscious you are about those experiences. Without your awareness of the world, the world will not exist for you.

On the other hand, attention means focusing this awareness that you have on the present. It often happens that you don't even pay attention to what you experience and perceive, which in itself is not even being aware. Attention means being aware and staying aware, being "there" through the moments that pass in succession. The remembering part is about remembering to pay attention and stay mindful, as it is easy to forget. You must remember to focus your awareness. This is mindfulness.

If you want to become mindful, you must be aware of all things as they happen around you. Remember to be present and give your full attention to be truly mindful, but this awareness must be clear and pure, without anticipation and prejudice, yet with good intentions. For mindfulness to truly be therapeutic, it must have goodness at the heart of it.

Why mindfulness?

Why is mindfulness becoming so popular now despite the fact that it's been in existence for years? Perhaps, the stressful life that people live nowadays is a big reason for this.

Lives full of deadlines, bills, schedules and appointments keep you from truly living in the moment. You live in anticipation of the next day, the next hour, forgetting how to truly appreciate the present as it happens.

On the other hand, there are those who live in the past. They are weighted down by regrets, anger and guilt over the mistakes and wrongs they caused others or others caused them months, years or even decades ago.

By being ever present, mindfulness helps you relieve yourself of stress, anxiety, depression and even physical pain.

The Concept of the Wisdom Mind

According to the Buddhist teachings that mindfulness is based on, all human beings have two minds - the wisdom and the ordinary mind. At the core of your being is the wisdom mind. It is pure and unchanging; it is simple and at peace, filled with hope and dignity.

Your wisdom mind knows your worth and core values and it retains them throughout your years. Your wisdom mind holds the goodness that is your essence. On the other hand, your ordinary mind is where all the negativity and adverse thoughts swirl and dance. Your ordinary mind surrounds your wisdom mind and clouds it with thoughts and ideas you've picked up through your life, and the troubled emotions that plague you. This ordinary mind clouds your wisdom mind and causes all your pain and suffering.

It is through mindfulness that your wisdom mind becomes clear to you again. Through mindfulness, you can do away with all the thoughts that cloud your wisdom mind, and instead, will allow you to be clearly aware and with intention.

Mindfulness Meditation

Mindfulness meditation is a special kind of meditation that has been clinically tested for its therapeutic potential. For those who are not familiar with meditation and how it works, it is basically about focused awareness.

Contrary to what a lot of people may think, meditation isn't about emptying your mind. Rather, it is about focusing your attention on one or two key aspects, such as your own breathing, a certain positive emotion, or even a word or phrase.

When it comes to mindfulness meditation, there are two types that you can choose from: formal or informal. A clarification is needed as the words meditative practice will often be at play, or even just the word practice. Practice here means the actual act of doing it, and doing it repetitively so that getting to a meditative state becomes easier for you. However, practice does not mean rehearsal. You cannot plan what you intend to do or give yourself deadlines and schedules. This is NOT living in the moment. Practice simply means doing it, and experiencing it. No more, no less.

Formal meditation is about intentionally giving time every day for meditation. This means taking the time out to really get deeper into mindfulness. Setting up a formal time to do your practice gives your body and mind enough time to prepare, making it easier to do. Formal meditation will allow you to understand more about how your own mind works, your habits and tendencies, how to develop curiosity and a sense of loving-kindness to all your experiences.

Informal meditation, on the other hand, is about getting into a meditative state of focused awareness while doing your daily chores or simply going about your day. Through continued practice of focused awareness, you can safely do any of your chores while in a meditative state. Chores such as cleaning, driving, cooking, and even talking to someone can all be done with focused awareness.

This way, you can continue to deepen your mental awareness without sacrificing your time. This also makes mindfulness meditation more accessible to you, and you can even do it more often, as you switch your brain toward focused awareness at any time of day.

Chapter 21: Formal Meditation

Advanced mindfulness, or "how to sit"

There are many, many ways to do formal sitting meditation. Different branches of Buddhist discipline promote different aspects of mindfulness, but since this book isn't really about Buddhism, we'll only consider here a very simple and straightforward breathing meditation.

Begin by sectioning off some time during the day where you know you won't be disturbed. Sit somewhere quiet (it doesn't have to be completely silent) and relatively comfortable. Get into position. You can sit cross-legged – no need for sitting lotus or half lotus position – or even lay flat on your back if you're sure you won't be falling asleep.

The point is to be comfortable but not to signal your body to sleep or "zone out." Relax all your muscles, including the ones of your face (do you ever notice how tight the jaw muscles can become?) and loosen the arms out of the shoulders so that they hang gently. Rest your hands on your knees or wherever comfortable. You could begin your meditation with some light stretching or yoga, if you like.

Your eyes can be closed or opened to a relaxed gaze on nothing in particular. Give yourself a few moments to become deeply aware of all the information coming in through your five senses. You can switch between them, as though you were shining the light of your consciousness on each separate element, or just let each sensation come into focus as it will.

Notice both inner sensations and stimuli from the outside. When it comes down to it, your inner thoughts and feelings have a very similar quality to fleeting noises outside, or a breeze blowing through the room, don't they? What's important here is to notice without attaching – don't notice and immediately assign any value ("that noise is so irritating" or "that warmth is so lovely"), just become aware. Just be.

Once you're comfortable with this, turn your consciousness to your breathing. Notice all the millions of tiny sensations associated with the process of in, out, in, out. Feel the temperature of the air, the sensation of it in every corner of your lungs, the way your ribcage stretches or rises as you inhale.

Your mind will start doing what it does best – conjuring up thoughts. Mountains of thoughts. When this "thought traffic" rushes in, acknowledge it and then let it go. Don't be self critical, just gently pull your awareness back to your breath. You're not trying to "think of nothing," you're just …being. You'll soon see that "just being" is remarkably difficult. Keep going!

You may grow bored, tired, irritated or distracted. At first, you may not be very skilled at maintaining focus for too long. But with practice, you'll enter into a mindful state more easily. Notice these feelings and let *them* go, too. Keep coming back to that clean, quiet, empty space within you. The strangely full and serene beauty of the present moment.

When you're ready, start moving and stretching a little and open your eyes to come out of your meditation. Some people like to finish off with more yoga or else a "walking meditation." It's up to you. If you journal, note how you feel after each session. You may notice that you develop fresh and unusual insights into problems you're experiencing, that you have a shifted perspective on your current challenges or that you feel a little more at peace or more joyful than usual.

Meditate every single day. The duration is not as important. Avoid using an alarm to end a session – it's often highly distracting. If you enjoy meditating, consider a longer formal retreat at a Buddhist center where you can go still for longer periods.

The benefits of being mindful

Practicing mindfulness can bring many benefits to your life.

Mindfulness makes you healthier

When you are aware of what's going on in your body, you know when it's distressed, and can help yourself sooner than if you were disconnected. You revel in healthful movement and you become more keenly tuned into how unhealthy substances affect you.

Mindfulness de-stresses you

Rushed, thoughtless action can lead to your body overproducing cortisol and adrenaline, which weakens your immune system, making it harder for you to heal from illness and injury, and hindering your cognitive abilities.

Mindfulness makes you a better friend, partner and parent

When you are mindful, you listen. You naturally become more empathic and considerate as you widen your awareness to include others. You are more compassionate and emotionally connected to others, and more aware of how your actions affect them. Plus, you're more relaxed and more fun to be around.

Mindfulness makes you more efficient

You can only solve problems you're aware of! If you're not constantly being derailed, distracted or overwhelmed, you work more intensely and purposefully – and you're likely get more satisfaction out of it.

Mindfulness makes you spiritually fulfilled

When you routinely ask yourself to become aware of how you respond emotionally to your world, you give yourself the opportunity to really strive for goals and create a lifestyle that actually serves you. What others think becomes less important as you become increasingly aware of your own inner values. You may discover relationships or situations that are actually making you unhappy, and give yourself the chance to pursue things that fulfil you on a much deeper level.

Mindfulness makes you more rational

Reactive people are pushed and pulled by the torrents of their emotions. They are "moody." But with mindfulness, you develop the ability to take a step back and disengage. You make decisions carefully and slowly, and can take in more information before you make those decisions.

Mindfulness makes you more creative

As we saw in a previous exercise, becoming mindful of the world of possibilities out there is often the first step to a creative, authentic response. Immerse in the richness of the present moment and you'll be amazed at how many novel, beautiful ideas there are to be found!

Building a mindful lifestyle

If you've slowly worked through each of these exercises and have taken the time to note your response to them, you may have noticed some patterns emerging. You may have developed a liking for one particular exercise or found that another didn't "work" for you at all. This is all vital information you can use in crafting your own personalized, mindful lifestyle.

For this section, try to pull together some of these ideas and get a more concise idea of what you can do now, with your life as it is, to become more mindful. What activities can you do every day? Which do you really enjoy?

- Consider making formal meditation a part of your life. Do it as often as you like, but every day is best. Commit to doing it. Then do it.

- Decide how you'd like to wake up every morning, and how you'll start each day. Some yoga for bodily awareness or a bit of journaling? A ritual where you immerse and invite your mind to focus?

- Make sure that you're scheduling regular, deep breathing into your life. Choose ways to include breathing into everything you do (sounds strange I know, but see how difficult it actually is!)

- If you journal, be aware that you're putting down thoughts and becoming conscious of them, rather than just encouraging the generation of more and more thoughts without reflecting on them.

- Add pleasurable, blissful elements to your life. Nature, music, sex, art, good food - it can be anything really. Train your consciousness to see bliss and joy in the ordinary things, too, and make more time in your life for things that make you happy.

- Regularly do "inventories." Track your progress. Is something working? No? Then drop it and try something else. Nothing is set in stone.

- Make your own rules. Decide on a meditation, ritual or habit that's all your own and personally fulfilling for you. Record your results.

Chapter 22: How To Practice Mindfulness.

Finally the chapter you read this entire book waiting for! In this chapter, I'd like to discuss some of the specific details of how a person can do a practical and effective mindfulness practice daily. I would like to build this from the ground up, starting with how you position yourself to how you breathe and discuss how you handle difficulties that may arise. Remember that the practices described here are basic mindfulness practices intended to help you start and become more interested in their practice. It is very difficult to "mess up" a mindfulness practice, with one exception… if we become acutely aware of our negative thinking and then choose to focus on those thoughts and feelings, we can make ourselves feel worse. This is highly inefficient and not equivalent to a good mindfulness practice. Instead, we will be allowing ourselves to let go of negative thinking and grow into healthier beings. I encourage you to fully read this and the following passages first before starting your practice as if will help you remain mindful if you have fewer distractions.

Positioning

How you sit is once again really up to you. Some traditional forms of mindfulness meditation sit in a lotus type position and hold their hands in certain ways. You are welcome to try this as well, knowing that when you start you may feel some discomfort that can help or hinder your mindful practice. More importantly, you should sit in a way that allows for deep breathing and full expansion of the lungs and chest. To accomplish this, sit with your back straight as if a string is pulling your head straight up in the air. Relax your arms and set them in your lap or in an open (not crossed) position. Relax your legs, regardless of where they lie, so if you are in a chair put your feet flat on the ground with your thighs parallel to the floor. I invite you to close your eyes, but if you aren't comfortable doing so, pick a neutral spot somewhere directly in front of you at eye level and try focusing on that. Lastly, make sure to breathe in through your nose and out through your mouth. With all this set up, you are now in a position for a mindfulness practice.

Just Breathe

Start by slowly counting to 4 as you breathe in. If you have not practiced this before, you may have to breathe with your chest and dig deep into your stomach for the last little bit, expanding your whole torso. Once you are full of fresh air, slowly control your out breath as you count to 5. You might, at first, let too much air out too fast. That's okay, you'll learn to control this process to slow yourself down. Now, once you reach the end of the out breathe, notice the natural pause that occurs between breaths and count to 4 without breathing. Repeat this for at least 1 minute, but for as long as you like. Some things that may help are to have a loudly ticking clock guide your in and out breaths, or to try and listen to your heart beat as a counter. There are also mobile apps that time you, including some apps that play musical notes for each in, out, and pause breath. Feel free to practice extending the times of your breaths, maybe even trying to reach a 10-15-10 breathing schedule!

Notice your bodily sensations as you breathe. Generations of eastern cultures have seen breath as an important part of psychological wellbeing. Ideas such as ki or chi, prana, and others all focus on the importance of breath as a part of life. Even the word spirit is derived from the Latin word "spiritus" which means breath. When we take deep breaths, we awaken our body and make it conscious of its own presence in the here and now. This present moment reminder helps us be less anxious because it takes our focus off the future and helps us be less depressed by taking our focus off the past. On a physiological level, deep breaths activate nerves in the lungs and body that help us control emotional reactivity, cools our body and our blood, and helps us circumvent our natural fight or flight responses activated by our nervous system. This causes improved blood flow to the brain and body, helping us feel lighter, calmer, and helps with decision making. All good reasons to make deep breathing a habit.

Thoughts

Now that you are breathing, let's examine thinking. At first, your mind will whirl with the usual thoughts of the day. "Am I doing this right?" "What's for lunch?" "This is ridiculous." All of these, and more, will try to enter your mind as your brain works on processing the day in the only way it knows how. When these thoughts arise, don't fight them. Instead, acknowledge them and bring your attention back to your breathing. I invite you to even thank your mind for having that thought, because having the thought proves your mind it alive! As you continue to practice this, your brain will get used to the idea of being quiet. When you have practiced this, you will have thoughts enter your mind and will be able to gently greet them and promptly coax them away from your awareness. One way to help you do this is to imagine the following as you practice (a sample of this can be found on my YouTube channel "Meaningful Therapist"):

Imagine you are in a great forest full of leafing trees. As you walk through the forest, notice the colors of the leaves, the smells of the soil and bark, and the sounds of life. As you do, allow yourself to notice the sound of a flowing stream nearby. Go to the stream, and stand on its bank. Once you are looking into the crystal clear waters of the stream, notice there are leaves gently floating on the surface of the water. Simply allow yourself to notice the leaves on the stream. As you do, you may notice thoughts enter your mind that you'd like to let go of. When those thoughts arrive, thank them for being there, not matter what they are, for they are your mind. Now, imagine you can pull that thought out of your mind. Hold the thought in your hand and describe to yourself. What is its shape, its form? What color is it? How big it is? It may be a word, or a character. Whatever it is, take the thought and place it on a leaf passing by on the stream. You'll see that the leaf will carry the thought and slowly it will flow down the stream and out of sight. Once it is out of sight, let it go out of mind. If it returns, simply repeat the process, letting it float away.

This is a guided meditation I learned from Dr. Steven C. Hayes when I was a student of his. His therapeutic modality, ACT (mentioned in the introduction), encourages you to get out of your mind and get back into your life. It has proven very helpful in getting clients to let go of invasive thoughts they believed were too overpowering.

Another way you can let go of thoughts is to distract yourself with a complex mindful task. Give this a try: Once you are in a mindful place, having done a few minutes of deep breathing and are seated comfortably, take a moment to imagine your whole body being colored in with a crayon. Don't go too quickly because it takes a very long time to color in a human sized area. Start at your toes, imagining you are an outline with a clear center, and color in each of your toes with a color of your choice. As you fill in more of the shape, move up your body and continue to color in all your parts. You can finish the exercise once you have colored in your whole head. Try visualizing the same with paint or with warm or cool sensations.

Focusing on this detail task requires a fair amount of mental power and can help distract the brain from over thinking and bring its attention to the here and now of your body, bringing you back to the present moment. Once again, you can use all of the parts of this book to familiarize yourself with How mindfulness works. This is by no means, nor is it intended to be, an exhaustive resource on mindfulness. Instead, this is a 5WH book intended to get you excited about mindful practices and motivate you to do your own research.

Chapter 23: Eating Mindfully

It has been said that we are what we eat. While it may not be totally accurate (eating pork knuckles doesn't make me a pig, right?), there is some truth to it. Generally speaking, eating junk results in junk-like productivity or health. Eat optimally and we can perform optimally.

In this chapter, let's take a look at some practical mindful eating habits worth acquiring.

Think First, Eat Later

By this I don't mean meditating before eating. What I mean is to pay more attention to what we eat. Often times, busy schedules are the single biggest hindrances to eating for optimal mental and physical performance and health. It's not surprising to discover that many of us rely on junk or highly processed foods for daily survival and performance. It's also not surprising to discover that many of us are stressed, anxious or even depressed as a result.

It's important to pay attention, think about or simply be mindful of the things we stuff inside our mouths. In particular, food and drinks that can jack us up big time and make us feel even more stressed, anxious and depressed. We must be careful to avoid or at least minimize consumption of the following if we'd like to successful manage our stress and anxiety levels:

Alcohol;

Coffee, cocoa, teas (except chamomile), energy drinks and other caffeine-rich drinks;

Fast food;

High sugar food items; and

Soda and other carbonated drinks.

Instead, be mindful to eat more of these for fighting off stress, anxiety and depression:

Avocados;

Bananas;

Chamomile Tea;

Fatty fish like sardines, salmon and tuna;

Milk; and

Swiss chard.

Also, keep in mind that generally speaking, whole and natural foods are much better compared to processed ones. And to help you choose better, simply ask yourself (or the food you're about to eat) this: how far is the final version from its original version. Simply put, can you still recognize that fried chicken as an actual part of a real chicken, unlike chicken nuggets or chicken hotdogs? If not, then it's highly processed and isn't helpful in the war against stress, anxiety and depression.

The Power Of Gratitude

The next time you eat, avoid the temptation to just dig your teeth in to bite the food. Try to think about how other people lovingly prepared the ingredients and cooked the food for you to enjoy.

From the farmer that grew the veggies to the market vendor who sold them to you and all the way to your spouse who lovingly whipped up a gastronomical feast – meditate on how much love they've put into the delicious food you're now enjoying.

Doing this may seem unnatural at first – and rightly so. Most – if not all – of us have been conditioned to not do so. With consistent practice however, it becomes easier and we become more thankful and content – two of the most powerful weapons in the war against depression, stress and anxiety. Why? It's because most of cases of depression, stress and anxiety have – to some degree – discontent and ingratitude as their root causes. So when we become more and more content and grateful, a big chunk of depression, stress and anxiety goes away.

Mind Your Emotions

Eating can either be a source of pleasure, pain or both. Eating too much can definitely be a source of depression, stress and anxiety because doing so can lead to obesity and serious health issues. And guess what? Emotions can seriously affect the way and how much we eat.

Emotional eating often leads to making extremely bad eating choices and habits such as eating highly processed and junk foods – and eating so much of them as well! Whether being too happy or sad, both extreme emotions can significantly increase our risks for eating really bad food (health wise), eating too much, or both!

So how can being aware or mindful of how we feel at the moment of eating help us win the battle against stress, anxiety and depression? To the extent that we know what emotions trigger bad eating decisions is the extent we can keep ourselves from reaching out to wolf down that box of dozen Krispy Kreme donuts with a liter of soda. The more we can do that, the healthier and fitter we can be, which can significantly reduce our stressors and depressors.

So how do we mind our eating emotions? It's very simple:

Pausing before eating, particularly if what's on the table is very unhealthy and is available in generous heaping amounts.

Think about how you're feeling at the moment – sad, angry, bored, anxious, excited or happy?

After knowing how you really feel prior to eating, ask yourself if you're really hungry – and be honest with yourself!

Often times, simply thinking about how we really feel prior to eating and whether or not we're really hungry is enough to keep us from overeating, especially when it comes to junk or processed foods. It allows to not just be truly mindful about what we eat but also lets us make consistently wise eating choices that contribute greatly to whether or not we feel stressed, anxious or depressed.

Relish The Taste

Did you know that by mindfully savoring your food's tastes, you could overcome stress, anxiety and depression? Yes, you can! As such, don't be all too excited to swallow your food as soon as you take a bite. Slowly and completely chew your food in order for you to really taste and relish your foods' delicious flavors.

Eating your food this way – silently and mindfully – you can cultivate the habit of eating healthy, which can be very helpful in winning the battle versus stress, anxiety and depression.

Chapter 24: Meditation To Increase Happiness

Meditation and mindfulness go hand in hand. Mindfulness refers to being present in the moment and ensuring that your mind is fully focused on a particular thing.

Here is a look at the connection between the two in detail.

It is believed that practicing mindfulness is a powerful way to combat suffering and increasing confidence and wisdom. Not only does it help increase your own wisdom but also influences people around you.

Mindfulness is often taught side by side with meditation in most Buddhist schools. It helps monks reach a higher level of inner consciousness.

Mindfulness can be used as a means to transport our minds to a place of calm. It is used to keep distractions at bay and increase focus on the current situation.

The human mind is prone to distractions and cannot focus on any one thing at a time. To resolve this, mindfulness tools and techniques can be employed.

It can be said that mindfulness does not move us into the opposite direction; rather it helps us get into a natural role. It teaches us to be present in the current moment and absorb the atmosphere that surrounds us. This helps reduce stress and controls anxiety to a large extent.

Mindfulness helps an individual go deep into their consciousness, thereby enhancing self-control. The mind does not wander and thus suffers less. A state of wakefulness helps to understand your surroundings better and curbs reactions such as anger, hate, jealousy and stress.

By being more present in your own self, you have the opportunity to go deep into your thoughts and draw from an in-built wisdom that lies within you. It has the potential to stop you from caving into negativity and prevent the onset of stress and anxiety.

You will feel more alive and in the moment. Your mind will not get easily distracted and will remain in one place, the place where you want your mind to remain. It is believed that most people tend to run away from current scenarios in the hope of getting to a better place. But doing so will only worsen the case and make it difficult for them to accept things. It is, therefore, best to indulge in mindfulness so that the situation is dealt with and does not lead to suffering.

Mindfulness is all about paying keen attention to the present moment. Paying attention to details makes it easier for a person to sort things out and be more present in the current situation. It is important to stay happy and in the moment.

When we become mindful, we tend not to be upset by small things in life. Our focus is fully on the current and what we are doing. Even if someone is trying their hardest to anger or upset you, you still do not get distracted and continue with your own work. If you think there needs to be a change in the setting, then it will automatically occur to you without having to put in too much thought or effort.

So how does one go about practicing mindfulness? Well, let us find out!

As mentioned earlier, mindfulness is all about being present in the current moment. You have to gather your thoughts and channel your positive energy.

To help you get started, here are some mindfulness exercises that you can take up on a day-to-day basis.

Mindful counting

One of the best and easiest mindfulness exercises is mindful counting. Mindful counting refers to counting up or down depending on how mindful you wish to become. Start from 0 and go all the way up to 60. Once done, go backwards from 60 all the way down to 0. Continue this until your mind is fully in the moment. This technique can help you combat stress and ensure that you are able to analyze the situation before taking action.

Mindful breathing

Mindful breathing refers to focusing on your breath. This is similar to Anulom Vilom except that you focus on your regular breath. Close your eyes and visualize your breath entering your nostrils and exiting. Ensure that you draw in a deep breath that originates from your stomach. You can count to 5 while focusing on your breath. If you do this for 5 to 10 minutes a day, then you will feel completely refreshed and your mind will feel energized. It can also help cut down on distractions and help focus on the task at hand.

Mindful meals

Eating is a very important part of life. We have to eat to live. Many people tend to rush through their meals and do not enjoy their food. It is important to avoid doing so as it can reduce the nutritional intake by your body. By indulging in mindful eating, you can bring your mind back into focus and enjoy your meals. It is imperative to spend at least 30 minutes per meal. Close your eyes while chewing your food. Concentrate on the flavors making sure you enjoy every aspect of the meal. Do this for all 3 meals.

Mindful exercise

Exercising is a vital part of life. If you do not exercise then your body starts releasing more cortisol as a response to stress. But through exercise, it is possible to increase the amount of serotonin in your body. It is best to engage in mindful exercising. Start by getting up early and stretching out your entire body. Go for a walk or go running. Maintain focus on the activity and the surroundings. If you have a pet, then walk him/her. Do not rush through the process and enjoy every aspect of it.

Mindful music

Music is one of the most natural stress busters in the world. By mindfully listening to music, you can do away with your stress and anxiety. Listen to mindful music and focus on the various beats. If you do not have the time to sit down and listen to music then put your headphones on while doing household chores and reel in peace.

Mindful showering

People have forgotten to appreciate the little things in life and are always in a hurry to fulfill some task or another. One great stress buster is taking a mindful shower. A shower not only helps to clean your body but also calms your mind down. Spend at least 30 minutes in the shower indulging yourself and remain fully focused on the activity. Start off by turning on the shower and visualize yourself being under a waterfall. Pick up the bar of soap and smell it to awaken your senses. Roll the bar over your body and focus on the trail it leaves behind. Lather up and take your time in washing it away. This experience can help you get over a stressful day.

Mindful cooking/chores

It is important to be mindful while cooking meals and performing daily chores. Do not indulge in watching television or having other distractions. You should be fully focused on the task at hand.

Mindful dreaming

Your dreams can tell you a lot about your subconscious mind. In fact, they hold the secret to why you might be going through stress and anxiety. In order to understand them better, it is best to engage in mindful dreaming. Repeat the phrase "I will remember my dream" 10 to 12 times before retiring to bed. It will help you remember your dream better in the morning. Maintain a book and pen to write down the dream as soon as you wake up. Try to find a pattern in your dreams so that you get a better idea of what is actually bothering you. Once you find out what is troubling you, you can work on solving the issue through meditation.

Chapter 25: How Your Thoughts Affect How You Feel

Have you ever experienced a difficult project or demanding task given by your management? What were your feelings and thoughts at that moment? Have you lost your coolness when deadline drew near? When you felt disturbed, what were your thoughts? Perhaps you did not notice them, but they are somehow connected in one way or another. The truth is that no matter how talented you are in any industries, there are anxieties which come with every endeavour you are required to undertake. Study shows that people who have a higher chance to be successful in their careers are those who have healthy self-esteem and displayed self-confidence at their workplace. Therefore, if you often have negative thoughts of self, such as self-worthlessness, they will affect the way you feel about yourself, and eventually will cost you your self-esteem and confidence. So, those negative thoughts and feelings must be dealt with. Our minds cannot differential between imagination and realty, it only able to differential between a thought and an emotion, and our thoughts will affect our feelings.

Mindfulness will be good for you if you have decided to build or enhance your self-confidence. Calmness, coolness and peace will be the ultimate effects of practising mindfulness. What mindfulness does is it helps you to see the event in your mind as it is, give attention to it without judging it and living in the present.

OTHER THINGS OF MINDFULNESS THAT YOU NEED TO KNOW

Mindfulness is Acceptance and Being, and Mindfulness is not Auto-pilot and Doing. When an event happened, one of those states (*Acceptance, Being, Auto-pilot* and *Doing*) may taking place inside or outside you that alarm you or distract you, but what they truly are? The meaning of *Acceptance, Being, Auto-pilot* and *Doing* are described as follows:

Acceptance

Acceptance is an essential part of mindfulness and it means that you will accept your feeling whether it is good or bad with no intention of altering or forcing them away.

Auto-pilot

Auto-pilot is the process of being absent in mind but present in body. It refers to those periods when we shift our attention away from things which we are familiar and doing daily; often we refer it as brainless task or unconscious act.

Mindfulness aim to help you to focus on everything you do and bring awareness to what you are performing at the present moment.

Doing and Being

The Doing is used to describe a situation when you lost yourself in whatever you are doing and may not respond to any changes around you, although this allows you to complete a task at hand without distraction at time, yet you may be stressed out and fill with anxiety in the process of the Doing.

Mindfulness helps you to be in the Being. Being yourself, doing your best with no self-judgemental; you accept your limitations and allows flexibilities in your current tasks and complete them with least stress. When there is a stress reduction, heart and mind will be able to sync in a much more balance way, confidence level will increase and you will response sensible with a clear mind instead of reacting to a disturbing situation.

IMPACTS OF MINDFULNESS

Mindfulness has been a modern practice of stress reduction management for the modern day in any office environment and any stressful circumstances; it is no longer a practice of a religion, for Mindfulness is commonly used clinically nowadays and it has proven to be beneficial for patients, who have anxiety disorders, and speed up their recovery.

Practising Mindfulness able to calm the mind and still the heart, it enhances self-esteem and self-confidence. There are also other positive impacts and they are:

Mindfulness is a skill which aids people to fulfil their dreams and live a life of satisfaction through awareness of one's needs and wants. It empowers people in preoccupy themselves with the completion of tasks in the present moment that may be contributed to their success and not wallow in worries for the future or dwell in regrets about failures in the past.

Mindfulness helps to improve the physical and emotional wellness of individuals. Studies show that the practice of Mindfulness can potentially help to reduce stress and boost the immune system. Generally, Mindfulness may cause you to live longer.

Mindfulness meditation helps to create a sound mind. It improves mental health by manage emotions like depression, anxiety, sorrow, hurt and so on via labelling and acknowledgement of those negative feelings.

Mindfulness has improved the quality of life for many and it is an important daily exercise for many, thus you may either choose mindfulness practice a priority or remain busy with things mindlessly everyday – it's all about your choice!

MINDFULNESS IN THE WORKPLACE

Mindfulness has always been the art of living in ancient days till modern medical science discovers its usefulness and helpful for assisting patients who struggling with Obsessive Compulsive Disorders (OCD), depression, anxiety disorders, such as phobias and panic attacks, and so on in the recent decade.

In the modern days, people practise mindfulness for stress reduction, enhance confidence and dealing with stress at workplace and any overwhelming situations to allows them to remain calm and compose to handle the troubling situation in a better way. Mindfulness has slowly integrated to the modern world as people often lost themselves in the virtual world, thus need to ground themselves, synchronise themselves with the reality, stay safe and vigilant with awareness of the surrounding and enjoy the present moment.

Recent studies reveal that mindfulness enhance self-confidence and this may be one of essential skills for a leader who want to excel in the workplace. Many organisations encourage their employees to practice mindfulness to reduce their work stress, stay healthy, build ability to handle difficult tasks and complete them. Mindfulness remains a good and simple practice for the well-being of a person in a complex situation to stay focus and calm.

There is no right or wrong emotion or feeling, nevertheless emotions can affect a person's productivity and work performance, therefore acknowledge and manage one's emotion is needful for whoever want to be professional and confidence at work.

Mindfulness exercises consist of identifying and acknowledging a feeling of oneself at present moment and allows the overwhelming feeling, such as anger, to slowly fading away. You may label the undesirable feeling when it appears and watch it subsides. You will feel that you are in control; self-confidence will come back once an undesirable feeling, such as anxiety, is gone.

Today's demands and expectations of an organisation towards an employee's work performance at one's workplace are stressfully high. It takes so much effort and time of an employee to impress an employer to secure their job as they have a family to feed; often employees are under pressure to deliver. All these pressures and enormous workloads will leave a person burn-out. A little moment to be mindful, meditate and calm your mind and heart may grant you a relieve from stressful moment, enable you to be more composed and collected in managing an overwhelming situation and to be more productive in work and life.

Mindfulness will produce a beneficial outcome for whoever practising it.

Chapter 26: Stepping Into The World

It is all very well to be positive and mindful within our own home but what about when we have to step into the big wide world and be surrounded by all different types of people and situations.

One of the more amazing things about the Universe is that it reflects what we hold within us. If we are in an unhappy state then we attract unhappy circumstances and people, therefore, we can literally use our surroundings as a guide to where we are in our vibration.

Finding your own Power

We have to find our own power within the hustle ad bustle of the world and it is actually this world that helps us find it. We see a lot of wanted ad unwanted in the world and it is exactly that, that makes us connect to our own power. When we see people who are unkind we can decide if we want to be like them or not. When we see people who go out of their way to help others we can decide if we want to make that part of us or not.

The way others treat us in this world is also vital. We may have people treating us poorly all the time but instead of focusing on that, focus on your own power. What is this teaching you? Some of the more gentle people are simply that because of being treated the opposite within their life somewhere. When we know how awful it is to be treated unkindly we natural treat others with pure kindness. These circumstances create great people. It is because of this world of contrast that we get to pick and choose who we want to be.

Finding your own Creativity

The Universe is always flowing to and through us and the way that we allow this and get in touch with this is through our creativity. Have you ever sat down and drawn something only to look at it and feel like it was never you who did such amazing work? Or maybe you've written something only to read it back and find that it's such great work, you could never have done that?

This is because your creativity is the Universe speaking through you and the more we connect to it, the more we feel it present in our everyday life. It is so important to always feel that connection because when we do, we get a sense of being protected or being looked after. Feeling like there is an almighty power that has your back is a wonderful way to live especially when you have to step into the world.

Being confident

Being confident with who we truly are can take time but once we get there, it's a place to stay. Confidence comes to us over time but it stems from a trust or a knowing that what we are doing with our lives is what is best for us and the more we trust that for ourselves, the more others will trust it too.

Allowing your inner self shine towards others

The more connected you are to the Universe and to yourself, the more you can connect with others around you. In you are a happy and positive person then that will shine onto them and inspire them to be the best that they can be too.

Allowing the world to work as it does

Accept that the world is working in fine order. You may not be able to see what happens behind the curtain but trust that what is meant to be, will be. When we try to interfere or make something happen then it only leads to frustration especially when we try to control others—we can only control what happens in our own life.

Simple Tips:

·Remind yourself that everything in the Universe is perfect

·Look for the things in the Universe that are working so well for you at the moment

·Be grateful for every situation and what it brings

·Use others as a guide to you as to who you want to be.

Chapter 27: Dealing With Concentration Issues

Many people perceive that meditation is the concentration or vice versa. But It is not so. In fact, Meditation helps you achieve concentration.

How to attain concentration?

Exercise and Meditation are the keys to improve concentration. There are many techniques that can help.

First thing first decide what you want to concentrate on.

It has often been noticed that you reflect what you perceive. You start impersonating someone's way of talking, walking or the way they eat in a matter of a couple of minutes just by concentrating on the act.

Avoid Multitasking.

It is always good to be proficient. But there is a difference between proficiency and multitasking. Being proficient means giving your best to complete a task. This is attainable through concentrating on one task at a time. The time you consume thereby is significantly less. Whereas when you multitask, you are distributing your attention on more than one activity and therefore you are not able to concentrate on one particular task. It increases the chances of errors and the amount of time consumed is high which in turn reduces your productivity.

So, you should ensure that whatever you do you should put your full heart and mind into it.

Practice Concentration

How can you practice concentration? It can be done by doing some exercises.

Sit in a place where you can be all by yourself. Practice focusing on an object. Stare at it continuously and find its intricacies.

Switch between complex and easy tasks

To not lose the track, it is always desirable to switch between tasks which demand less focus and the ones that demand high focus.

Playing call of duty requires much more attention than watching a movie. When you toggle between such tasks, you contemplate the tasks better.

The power of concentration is immense. It helps to retain even the trivial details. Once you attain the power of deep concentration, it will bear fruitful results for you.

In today's overcrowded media environment, Attention is hard to find. You may be selling information, goods or your ideas, everything needs Attention. So how can you capture somebody's interest?

When you can do the common things of life uncommonly, you will command the attention of the world. - George Washington Carver

1. Storytelling: The best way to hold Attention is by Storytelling. One has to stimulate creative insights or innovation and hold on to it by keeping the focus with

a powerful storyline. The younger generation believes in getting triggered by actions which allow the brain to focus on a single thing and thus hold Attention. For instance, when playing a video game, one is glued to the screen for endless minutes or hours playing without getting distracted. These games continually trigger the orienting response, keeping the user's attention glued to the screen. Through Storytelling, you can immediately connect with people by including them in the story and consequently have the power to convince your message. Use your emotions and make it personal.

"The most basic way to get someone's attention is this: Break a pattern." -Chip Heath

2. Quality Content: Another method to grab attention is through Content. "Content is the King". Publish only good quality and useful content. A useful benefit must be associated with good reading and using your content should be beneficial to the reader. Focus on the

quality and keep in mind the target audience for whom the content is prepared. If content expands to an unrelated topic, then the attention is diverted, so keep track of the audience in mind. As far as possible, include the current events or news that is useful to the reader and follow the age-old KISS principle "Keep It Simple, Stupid". Content should be conveyed directly in an easy to understand format rather than using fanciful words. A confused mind does not pay attention.

3. Make others turn around: If someone fires a gun, you are bound to turn around, or if a female walker wears red, she is more likely to be picked up. Similarly, find ways to play on people's instincts to get Attention. Not necessarily by shouting, but maybe by treating your customers with a warm coffee might help in getting them to notice.

4. Mystery: Have you ever wondered why we're unable to put down a good book or stop watching an engrossing movie? Our

memory is fine-tuned to remember incomplete stories, and we also dislike uncertainty. So we try to reduce it by any means possible, and you can use this to your advantage. For instance, tell a client or assign yourself a task that you will complete it, only when he does. This compulsion to complete will nag him, and you have got that Attention.

5. Reward: Rewards that we can touch, experience, or even visualize have a greater impact on our attention. Like, if the incentive is a party, then instead of saying it, if you could send pictures of delicious food and the ambiance, it would grab instant Attention.

6. Disruption: People often tend to pay attention when expectations are violated. The more disruptive the thing is, the more interesting it becomes. Do the unexpected or surprise them. For instance, beat the deadline that is very difficult, call a friend or colleague for a walk instead of coffee, etc.

7. People consistently rate experts as the most trusted persons than any celebrity. It is believed that if an expert gives advice, then the person who is listening, blindly follows him because the brain slows down as to the decision-making and makes him feel that the expert is always right. So the credentials, their expertise in the field and their reference as to the knowledge about the topic at hand are all absorbed with full Attention.

8. Repetition: If you believe in passing a message, then try repeating it. Exposing the subjects to the same statement may make them believe it.

It is a common phenomenon where children remember things that are often repeated and so also adults are more prone to see a thing or an advertisement which is repeated over and over again.

9. Acknowledgement: Create a feeling that you care about them and this feeling will capture their interest, and they will repay you. All mammals need attention, but human beings are the only ones who need

acknowledgment. So give them the sense of belonging to a community that cares about them, and you are bound to get that much-desired Attention.

Attention can be grabbed in as less than 8 seconds, and it can extend to more than an hour. Getting people to listen to you is an art and has to be dealt with sensitively. Adult attention has diminished in the recent years, but can be revived with these useful points that can hold the attention span for a longer period.

Conclusion

Thank you again for downloading this book!

I hope this book was able to help you to learn about meditation

The next step is to start meditating to enjoy the amazing benefits of meditation. It is important to start small instead of starting with 30 minutes of meditation, start with 5 minutes, and build this up. This will avoid instances where you feel that meditating is too overwhelming making you abandon the practice.

Thank you and good luck!

www.ingramcontent.com/pod-product-compliance
Lightning Source LLC
Chambersburg PA
CBHW072002070526
44583CB00015B/1298